Contents

KT-118-166

4   Exploring the Web   65

5   Intermediate browsing   97

INTERNET EXPLORER 5

in easy steps

Mary Lojkine

COMPUTER STEP

In easy steps is an imprint of Computer Step
Southfield Road . Southam
Warwickshire CV33 OFB . England

Tel: 01926 817999 Fax: 01926 817005
http://www.computerstep.com

Notice of Liability
Every effort has been made to ensure that this book contains accurate
and current information. However, Computer Step and the author shall
not be liable for any loss or damage suffered by readers as a result of
any information contained herein.

Trademarks
Microsoft® and Windows® are registered trademarks of Microsoft
Corporation. All other trademarks are acknowledged as belonging to
their respective companies.

Printed and bound in the United Kingdom

ISBN 1-84078-036-3

Getting started

Before you can make use of Internet Explorer, you need to get connected to the Internet. This chapter explains what that means and outlines your options. It then shows you how to obtain, install and run Internet Explorer.

Chapter One

Covers

Introduction to the Internet

 This book is in three sections. Chapters 1-4 cover the things you need to know to start making use of Internet Explorer. Chapters 5-8 cover more advanced features. Chapters 9-10 explain how to use Outlook Express, the mail and news program supplied with Internet Explorer.

The Internet is a 'network of networks' that connects computers from all around the world. It's estimated that over 100 million people use the Internet, and the number increases every day.

You can use the Internet to access the latest news; research almost any topic you can imagine; shop for products and services; or get information about your favourite sport or pastime. You can also send messages to your friends, participate in discussion groups and obtain software for your computer.

History of the Internet

The Internet has its roots in 1969, when the US Government decided to connect some of its computers together so scientists and military agencies could communicate more easily. The system was designed to be very robust, so there was no central control centre. Each machine operated independently and messages travelled by whatever route seemed most convenient at the time.

In the 1970s several more computer networks were established by military and academic institutions. Eventually many of these networks were linked together, creating the network of networks we now know as 'the Internet'. During the 1980s the Internet was dominated by scientists, academics, computer experts and students, but the user-friendly software of the 1990s has encouraged a much wider range of people to make use of it. By the end of the 2000s you'll be taking it for granted.

Although some parts of the world are better represented than others, the Internet is becoming a truly global phenomenon. You can connect to a computer in Australia or New Zealand as easily – and as cheaply – as to one just down the road.

No-one owns or controls the Internet, although there are various organisations that endeavour to keep everything running smoothly. It can be creaky, cranky and intensely irritating, but for the most part it works remarkably well.

The World Wide Web is not the same thing as the Internet. The Internet is a network of computers. The Web is a service that uses the Internet to transfer information from one place to another. Other services include e-mail (Chapter 9) and newsgroups (Chapter 10).

The World Wide Web

The recent surge of interest in the Internet is due to the World Wide Web. Developed in 1990 at CERN, the European Laboratory for Particle Physics, the Web consists of millions of magazine-style pages. Unlike pages in a printed magazine, however, Web pages can include sound samples, animations, video clips and interactive elements as well as text and pictures.

Web pages are connected together by 'hypertext' links – electronic cross references that enable you to jump from page to page by clicking on underlined text or highlighted images. A page stored on a computer in London might have links to pages stored in Moscow, Tokyo and Washington, which in turn might be linked to pages in many other countries. The result is a network of connections stretching right around the globe – hence 'World Wide Web'.

You don't need to know where any of the pages are, because you can follow the links. However, if you know the address of the page you want to view, you can jump straight to it.

Turn to Chapter 4 for more information about a selection of the most popular pages on the Web.

Anyone can create a Web page, so there's a huge range of material to explore. Government departments, museums, and educational institutions are pouring information on to the Web, and many companies use it to promote their products or sell directly to the public. Publishers and broadcasters produce on-line magazines and news services, and you'll find many pages dedicated to the hobbies and interests of private individuals.

Web browsers

In order to look at – or 'browse' – Web pages, you need a piece of software called a 'Web browser'. It enables you to find Web pages and display them on your screen.

Internet Explorer is Microsoft's Web browser. It's a good choice for beginners because it's free and easy to use. It comes with a companion program called Outlook Express that enables you to send messages and join discussions, plus a host of other programs for expert users.

Connecting to the Internet

Before you can access the Web, you need to be connected to the Internet. There are three possibilities: your company or university may provide a direct connection; you can visit a cyber café or public library; or you can use a modem (a device that enables computers to communicate with each other over a phone line) to connect your home computer to the Internet.

Company connections

 The rest of this chapter assumes you're using a modem to connect to the Internet (see opposite). If you are connecting via a university or company network, ask your systems manager to help you install and configure Internet Explorer.

If you are at university, or work for a large company that has an internal computer network, you may already be connected to the Internet. Ask your systems manager if it's possible for you to access the World Wide Web from your PC, Macintosh or workstation.

The advantage of a company connection is that you don't have to pay for it. There are several disadvantages: you have to be at work to access the Internet; there may be rules about what you can use it for; and you have no control over the speed of the connection, which can be anything from excellent to awful.

Cyber cafés, pubs and libraries

The cyber café is the Internet equivalent of the public telephone, but generally warmer and more comfortable. You can drink coffee (or beer, in a cyber pub) and use the café's computers to explore the Internet. Most charge by the half hour or hour, and the rates are quite reasonable. Your local library may also have computers you can use.

If you aren't sure whether the Internet is for you, paying to use someone else's equipment for a few hours is a good way to find out. You don't have to worry about setting up the software, and there's usually someone to help with any problems. However, you may not have access to the full range of Internet services – for example, you may not be able to send and receive e-mail.

Dial-up connections

The most versatile option is to use a modem to connect your own computer to the Internet. Regrettably, this is also the option that requires the most input – both financial and technical – from you.

You need five things to establish a dial-up connection:

1   A computer. Internet Explorer is available for PCs, Apple Macintoshes and Unix workstations, but this book concentrates on the version for PCs running Windows. You will need at least a 66MHz 486 with 16Mb of RAM and 50–150Mb of free hard-disk space. A faster, more powerful computer with more RAM will make browsing more enjoyable.

 V.90 modems don't actually run at 56kbps – that's their theoretical top speed. In reality, they operate at 45–50kbps.

2   A modem. Modems come in two flavours – internal and external – and a range of speeds. It's a false economy to buy a modem with a top speed of anything less than 56kbps (kilobits per second). Modems that conform to the V.90 standard will run at this speed. Slower modems may be cheaper, but you'll run up bigger phone bills.

3   A telephone line. If your phone company offers cheap deals on local calls, so much the better.

4   An Internet service provider (see page 12). A service provider has a computer system that is permanently connected to the Internet, and to a bank of modems. You use your modem to connect to one of your service provider's modems, via your telephone line, thereby making your computer (temporarily) part of the Internet.

5   Connection software (see page 15). You'll need to install the Dial-Up Networking utility supplied with Windows to connect to the Internet.

Internet service providers

Internet service providers (ISPs) enable you to connect to the Internet via a modem and telephone line. Most also provide basic software and have technical-support people to help you with any problems. There are two types: regular service providers and on-line services.

Unless your telephone line is supplied by a company that offers free local calls, you'll also be running up your phone bill while you're connected to the Internet.

Regular service providers such as BT Internet, Demon Internet, Direct Connection and Pipex Dial exist primarily to provide connections. They charge a flat monthly fee, no matter how much (or how little) time you spend on-line. You may also be charged a one-off start-up fee that covers the cost of setting up your account and supplying you with Internet software.

The Internet service provider market is very competitive, so many companies offer additional services that you may find useful. Look out for extras such as e-mail addresses for all the family; access to a games server; global roaming so you can access the Net while you're working overseas; and reception or forwarding of faxes.

Many service providers offer one-month free trials for new users. They're a good way to find out what you'll get for your money. If you decide not to continue, you must ring up and close your account before the trial ends. If you don't, you'll be liable for the monthly charges.

On-line services – AOL, CompuServe, LineOne and the Microsoft Network (MSN) – provide the same services as regular ISPs, and also have subscriber-only content and private discussion forums. This was a big plus in the days when there weren't many reliable news services on the Web, and business users may still find that some on-line services offer information that isn't available elsewhere. In general, though, the Web has grown so much that you no longer need to pay extra for subscriber-only content.

Most of the on-line services charge a fixed monthly fee, and they usually cost a bit more than regular service providers. Some also offer low-user plans with a reduced monthly fee that only covers your first few hours on-line. Once you've used up your monthly allotment, you're charged by the hour – and you can run up substantial bills if you end up using the Internet more than you expected.

You're probably thinking that there doesn't seem to be much difference between regular service providers and on-line services. You're correct: a few years ago they were poles apart, but now they offer very similar deals. The main remaining difference is that each on-line service has its own software. They all give you a customised version of Internet Explorer for browsing the Web, but most have special software for connecting to the Internet and sending e-mail messages. In contrast, a regular service provider will let you use whatever software you fancy, and is a better bet if you like experimenting with different programs.

Free services

There are a number of service providers that don't charge a monthly fee. Instead, they take a percentage of your phone-call charges. You don't pay any extra for your calls; your phone company just makes a bit less, because it passes on some of the money to the service provider. However, you are charged a premium rate if you have problems and need to call the technical-support line.

Apart from free technical support, free services provide all the things you'd expect from a regular service provider, including access to the Web and e-mail accounts. However, they tend to be less reliable – you may have difficulty getting connected because all the lines are engaged, or you may find that everything gets very slow at busy times.

Free services offer a very good deal if you're reasonably comfortable with computers and don't mind if you can't get connected 100 per cent of the time. If you think you're going to need some help getting to grips with your new Internet software, you're better off with a regular service provider that will provide as much technical support as you require at local-call rates. Just don't know? Signing up with a free service is an easy, no-commitment way to get a look at the Internet. If you like what you see, but find you're spending a lot of money on technical-support calls, you can switch to a regular service provider or an on-line service.

Once you've decided what type of service provider you require, you need to settle on a particular service. Most Internet magazines publish lists that you can refer to. The things to consider when choosing a provider are:

1   Level of service. Make sure you'll be getting full Internet access, including e-mail, newsgroups and the Web. Find out what software is supplied, especially if you're considering an on-line service, and whether you can use something else if you don't like it. If you're planning to create your own Web pages, ask about free Web space.

2   Access numbers. Most service providers use special 'Lo-call' phone numbers that are charged at the same rate as a local call, no matter where you call from. If you're considering one that doesn't, make sure it has a number within your local-call area.

3   Modem speed. Make sure your service provider supports the fastest speed your modem can manage.

4   Subscriber-to-modem ratio. If you choose a service provider that has a lot more subscribers than modems, you'll find it hard to get through. Aim for a ratio of around 15 subscribers per modem (15:1).

5   Technical support. Find out how much you'll be charged for calls to the helpline, and check the opening hours – a helpline that is only available during the day won't be much good if you're expecting to use the Internet after work or at the weekend. If you don't have much experience with computers, call up and ask a few questions. If the service provider can't answer them clearly, try someone else.

Dial-Up Networking

These days getting on the Internet usually just involves installing your service provider's software pack. You don't actually need to understand how the connection software works, and you can skip to page 17 if you aren't interested.

Establishing a connection

Before you can use Internet Explorer, or any other Internet application, you need to persuade your modem to connect your computer to the Internet. You do this by running a small program called Dial-Up Networking, which stores your service provider's details and controls your modem.

As well as handling the connection, Dial-Up Networking establishes a TCP/IP interface, enabling other programs to send and receive data. TCP/IP stands for Transmission Control Protocol/Internet Protocol, and it's the common language of the Internet.

How the Internet works

Every computer on the Internet has a unique address, or 'IP number', which looks something like `194.88.75.43` The more important ones also have names, such as `www.computerstep.com` The Domain Name System (DNS) converts the easy-to-remember names into computer-friendly numbers when you type in an address.

TCP and IP are responsible for getting data from one address to another. TCP breaks it up into small 'packets' and adds the address, then IP gets the packets to their destination, using any available route. At the other end, TCP checks that all the packets have arrived and reassembles them in the correct order.

If there's a problem somewhere along the way, the packets are rerouted to avoid it. They might not all take the same route, and some packets go missing and have to be re-sent, but everything should get there in the end – without any help from you. What you will notice is that packets don't arrive in a steady stream. You often get a bunch of packets, and then a gap, and then another bunch, and so on.

...cont'd

If you need to install Dial-Up Networking yourself, click the Start button and go to Settings>Control Panel. Double-click the Add/Remove Programs icon, click the Windows Setup tab and find Dial-Up Networking in the Components list – it should be under Communications. Select it, click OK twice and follow the on-screen instructions.

Installing and using Dial-Up Networking

Your service provider's disc will check whether Dial-Up Networking is installed on your PC. If it isn't, the setup routine will ask you to insert your Windows CD so it can install it for you.

1. To open Dial-Up Networking, click the Start button and select Programs>Accessories. You'll find the program here, or in the Communications subsection. You should see a Make New Connection icon and an icon for your service provider.

2. To add an icon for another service provider, double-click here and follow the on-screen instructions. Alternatively, run the Internet Connection Wizard – see page 21.

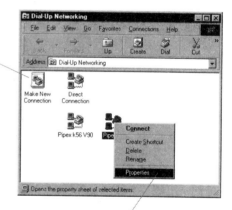

Dial-Up Networking is often shortened to 'DUN', and you'll sometimes see the service provider icons referred to as 'DUN connectoids'.

3. To connect to your service provider manually, double-click its icon (normally Internet Explorer will do this for you).

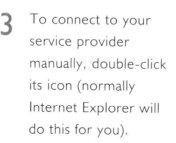

4. If your service provider's phone number changes or you buy a new modem, right-click your service provider's icon and select Properties to enter the new details.

Obtaining Internet Explorer

Internet Explorer 5 is included with all editions of Microsoft Office 2000.

Most service providers include a copy of Internet Explorer in their start-up package. You can also order it directly from Microsoft, and you'll often find it on the CDs attached to the front of computer magazines. If you've only just bought your PC, you'll probably find that Internet Explorer has been preinstalled by the manufacturer.

If you're already an Internet user, you can download Internet Explorer from Microsoft's Web site. You'll need plenty of patience, though – a 'typical' installation takes over an hour to download.

'Download' means to copy a file from a computer on the Internet to your computer. Uploading a file copies it from your computer to one on the Internet.

1 Connect to Microsoft's Web site at:
`http://www.microsoft.com/windows/ie/`

2 This page changes regularly, but it's always linked to the download area.
Look for a 'Download Now' button or heading. Click it to move to the download pages.

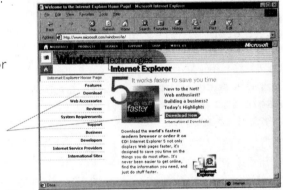

3 Follow Microsoft's on-screen instructions to download the Internet Explorer setup program.

4 When the setup program has been copied on to your hard disk, follow the instructions on pages 18–20. When you get to Step 13, the setup program will download the rest of the Internet Explorer files and install them for you.

Installing Internet Explorer

If you're installing Internet Explorer from a disc supplied by your service provider, follow whatever instructions have been provided. They will include details of any service-specific settings or options.

If you're installing Internet Explorer from a magazine's cover-mounted CD, or have ordered a CD from Microsoft, you'll get a menu screen when you insert the disc. Look for an 'Install Internet Explorer 5' option and click it to start the setup program.

If you're using a service provider's setup disc, some screens may look slightly different, and there may be extra steps where you're prompted to enter personal details such as your name and preferred e-mail address.

1 The Wizard helps you install Internet Explorer. Click here to accept the licence agreement.

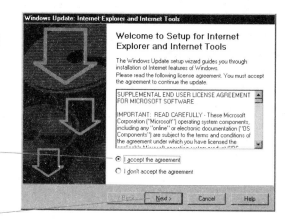

2 Click Next to proceed.

3 Select 'Typical' for a basic installation with the most useful add-ons. Click Next and go to Step 13.

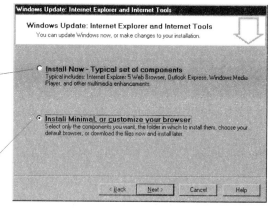

4 Select 'Minimal, or customize...' to decide which components should be installed. Click Next to proceed.

...cont'd

Not sure what a component does? Click on its name to select it and a brief description will appear on the right.

5 Select Minimal, Typical or Full as a starting point.

6 Click the checkboxes to add or remove components.

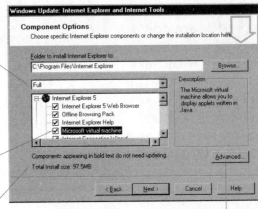

Some items may already be installed on your PC. If so, their names are shown in bold. You don't need to install them again.

7 The amount of hard-disk space required is shown here.

8 Click Advanced for three more options.

9 This option is for people who have several Web browsing programs.

10 This option is for Web designers who want to see how their pages look in Internet Explorer 4.

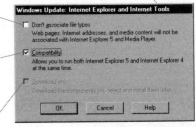

Selecting the 'Download only' option means you have a backup of the installation files and can reinstall Internet Explorer 5 if there's a problem in the future.

11 This option will be available if you're downloading Internet Explorer (see page 17). Select it to copy the files on to your hard disk instead of installing the program straight away.

12 Click OK to go back to the screen shown in Step 5, then click Next to proceed.

...cont'd

 If you are down-loading Internet Explorer, the setup program will auto-matically connect to the Internet and fetch all the files.

13 Wait while the setup program installs all the components you've selected. It takes several minutes to install Internet Explorer from a CD.

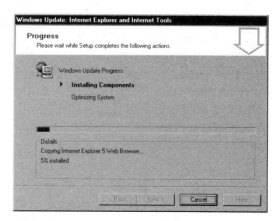

14 When you see this screen, click Finish to restart your computer.

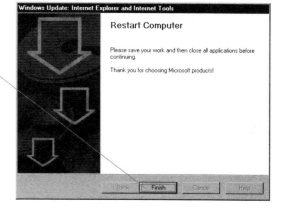

 If you have been using Internet Explorer 4, your icon will be in the same place as before. However, it will now run Internet Explorer 5.

15 When your computer restarts, you will have an Internet Explorer icon on your desktop.

Internet Explorer

Internet Connection Wizard

The Internet Connection Wizard makes it easy to enter the details of your Internet account.

If you are using a service provider's setup disc, you won't need to run the Wizard (although some of its screens may pop up during the installation process), and you can skip to page 23. The Wizard is useful if you have to set up an account manually, perhaps because you've bought a new computer and can't find your old setup disc.

You will need to know: your service provider's phone number (the modem number, not the one you call to talk to someone); your user name and password, your e-mail address and the addresses of your service provider's mail servers. Your service provider will give you these details.

You can also run the Wizard from Internet Explorer. Go to Tools> Internet Options and click the Connections tab, then click Setup.

1 Go to the Start menu and select Programs>Accessories> Communications> Internet Connection Wizard. Answer the questions, clicking Next after each step.

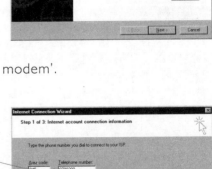

2 Select the third option.

3 Select 'I connect through a phone line and modem'.

4 Enter the phone number you use to connect to your service provider.

5 Enter your user name and password.

6 Enter a name for the connection. The name of your service provider will do nicely.

7 You'll then be prompted to set up your e-mail account.

8 Enter your name.

9 Enter your e-mail address.

10 Unless you've been told otherwise, set the server type to POP3. Enter the addresses of your service provider's mail servers.

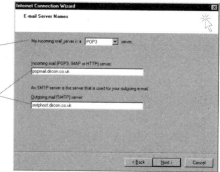

11 Enter your user name and password. Usually these will be the same as before, but some service providers give you different ones for e-mail.

12 That's all there is to it!

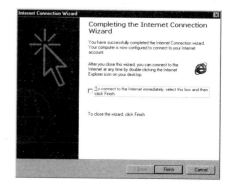

Running Internet Explorer

To run Internet Explorer, double-click its icon or select it from the Programs section of the Start menu.

Opening a connection to the Internet is often referred to as 'logging on'. Likewise, 'logging off' means closing the connection.

If you tell your computer to save your password, anyone with access to it can connect to the Internet.

If you select 'Connect automatically', you won't need to click the Connect button in future.

1 If your computer is not set up to connect to the Internet, the Internet Connection Wizard will run – see page 21.

2 Most service provider's setup discs sort out the connection for you, so you're more likely to see a log-on screen.

3 Enter your user name and password.

4 If you want your computer to remember your password, select this checkbox.

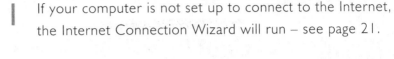

5 Click the Connect button. You should hear your modem dial and connect. You'll see messages describing its progress at the bottom of the dialogue box.

6 Internet Explorer will display a Web page like this, or possibly a page from your service provider's Web site.

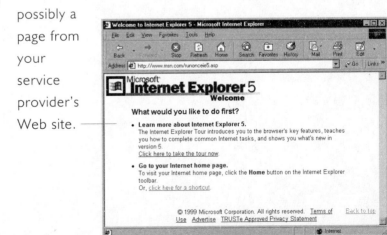

...cont'd

7 You're now ready to go to Chapter 2 and learn how to browse the Web.

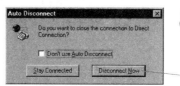

8 When you close Internet Explorer, you'll be prompted to close the connection. Click Disconnect Now.

The System Tray is a sunken area at the right-hand end of the Windows Taskbar.

9 To disconnect without closing Internet Explorer, go to the System Tray and look for an icon showing two computers connected together. Double-click it.

10 Click the Disconnect button to log off.

Fine-tuning your connection

Your connection settings determine how and when Internet Explorer connects to the Internet. You can alter them to make sure it only connects when you want it to, and disconnects automatically when the connection is idle.

You can change your settings from Control Panel, too. Double-click the Internet Options icon to access the dialogue box shown here.

1 Go to Internet Explorer's Tools menu and select Internet Options. Click the Connections tab.

2 Click Add to enter Dial-Up Networking settings (see page 15) for a second service provider.

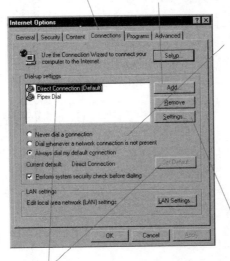

3 Select 'Never dial...' to make all connections manually using Dial-Up Networking. 'Always dial...' enables Internet Explorer to make connections as required and is the best choice.

To use a connection other than the default one, select it from the drop-down list at the top of the log-on screen (see page 23) before you click Connect.

4 If you have accounts with several service providers, all the possible connections will be listed here. Tell Internet Explorer which one to use by selecting it and clicking Set Default.

5 To fine-tune a connection, select it and click Settings. This opens the dialogue box shown overleaf.

...cont'd

A proxy server stores copies of all the Web pages that have been viewed by people who use your service provider. If there's a copy of the page you want to see, Internet Explorer can download it from the proxy server more quickly than it could fetch it from the original Web site. Using a proxy server is like having a giant Temporary Internet Files folder (see page 141) that you share with all your service provider's other customers.

6 If your service provider has a proxy server, enter the details here.

7 If your user name or password changes, update your details here.

8 Click Properties if your service provider's phone number changes or you install a new modem. You can also amend these details from Dial-Up Networking.

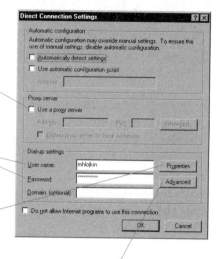

9 Click Advanced for further options.

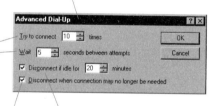

10 If all your service provider's modems are busy, Internet Explorer will redial. Specify how many times it should try and how long it should wait between attempts.

11 Select 'Disconnect if idle...' to drop the line if you don't seem to be doing anything.

The 'Disconnect' options ensure you don't run up a big phone bill if you get distracted. In both cases you get a warning before you're cut off.

12 Select 'Disconnect when connection may no longer be needed' to drop the line if you've closed all your Internet programs.

13 Click OK three times to finish.

Basic Web browsing

This chapter shows you how to enter Web addresses and jump from page to page. It also explains what to do when you encounter images, sounds, video clips and program files. Finally, you'll learn how to save and print Web pages.

Chapter Two

Covers

Introducing Internet Explorer

Like most Windows programs, Internet Explorer has title, menu and tool bars across the top of the window, and a status bar at the bottom. The most important areas of the screen are:

Title bar – displays the name of the page.

Menu bar.

Standard buttons.

Address bar – displays the address, or URL, of the page.

Service providers sometimes customise Internet Explorer, so your version may look slightly different.

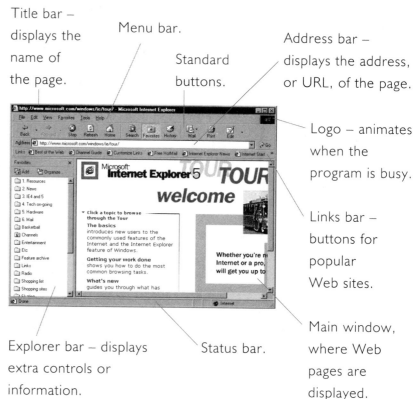

Logo – animates when the program is busy.

Links bar – buttons for popular Web sites.

Main window, where Web pages are displayed.

Explorer bar – displays extra controls or information.

Status bar.

Customising the toolbars

You can rearrange the Menu bar, Standard buttons, Address bar and Links bar, or turn some of the bars off to increase the size of the main window.

You can also turn toolbars on or off from View> Toolbars.

1 To turn off a toolbar, right-click on an empty section of any bar. Deselect the toolbar you no longer wish to display.

2 To move a toolbar, use your mouse to grab the grey handle at the left-hand end. Drag it up, down or across.

3 You can have several bars on the same line.

Another way to increase the screen area is by selecting View>Full Screen. If this mode is too minimalist for you, right-click on the Standard buttons to add some of the other toolbars.

4 To expand a bar to its full width, double-click on its handle. Double-click again to put it away.

5 The toolbars have to be at the top of the window – you can't move them to the side or the bottom or turn them into floating tool palettes.

Customising the Standard buttons

As you become more experienced, you may want to change the toolbar buttons. You can add buttons for more advanced features, or remove the ones you don't use. You can also remove the text and reduce the size of the buttons to create a more compact toolbar.

1   To customise the Standard buttons, right-click on an empty section of the toolbar. Select Customize.

Separators are grey lines that can be used to divide the toolbar into sections. Add as many as you need to keep your toolbar tidy.

2   To add a button, select it from this list and click Add.

3   To remove a button, select it from this list and click Remove.

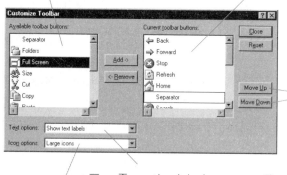

4   To change the order of the buttons, select one and click Move Up or Move Down.

5   Turn the labels on or off.

If you select 'No text labels' and 'Small icons', your toolbar will look a lot like the toolbars in Microsoft Office.

6   Choose large or small icons.

7   Click Close to finish, or Reset to undo all your changes.

Understanding addresses

Chapter 4 contains a selection of URLs for you to try.

Once you're comfortable with the interface, you're ready to go somewhere. Every page on the Web has a unique address, otherwise known as a Uniform Resource Locator (URL). You've probably seen some Web addresses in newspapers and magazines and on television.

The URL for Microsoft's Internet Explorer Tour is:

A page is a single Web document. Some are quite long – use the scroll bar to move down them. A site is a collection of related pages, and the server is the computer on which all the docu-ments are stored.

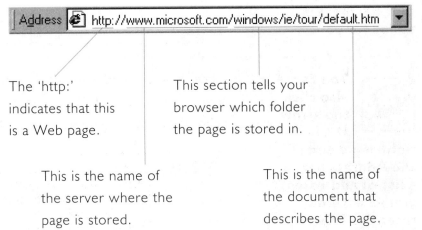

The 'http:' indicates that this is a Web page.

This section tells your browser which folder the page is stored in.

This is the name of the server where the page is stored.

This is the name of the document that describes the page.

Most server names end in .com **(commercial),** .org **(organisation) or** .net **(Internet). UK-specific servers have names ending in** .co.uk, .org.uk **or** .net.uk **instead. Other countries have their own two-letter codes.**

Unless you tell it otherwise, Internet Explorer assumes you are looking for a Web page, so you don't have to type the http:// at the beginning. If you're looking for the main page of a company's site, you can also leave out everything after the first single slash. To locate the main page of Microsoft's Web site, for example, you would enter: www.microsoft.com

Other addresses

You will also see URLs for other types of Internet site:

URL begins	Type of site
ftp:	FTP site (see page 111)
https:	Secure Web site (see page 135)
mailto:	e-mail address (see page 148)
news:	Usenet newsgroup (see page 174)

Entering an address

If you type 'computer-step' (omitting the hyphen) and press Ctrl+Enter, the rest of the address is added for you.

If you know the address of the Web page you wish to visit, you simply enter it into Internet Explorer. There are three ways to do this:

1 Type the address into the Address bar, then click the Go button or press the Enter key. Internet Explorer will find and display the page.

Address	www.computerstep.com	▼	↻ Go

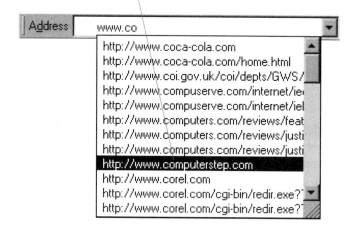

You can also click the arrow at the right-hand end of the Address bar for a list of addresses you've entered recently. This list only shows addresses you've typed yourself.

2 Once you've visited a few sites, Internet Explorer tries to anticipate your typing. If you see the right address in the drop-down list, click on it. You don't have to press Enter.

Address	www.co	▼

http://www.coca-cola.com
http://www.coca-cola.com/home.html
http://www.coi.gov.uk/coi/depts/GWS/
http://www.compuserve.com/internet/ie
http://www.compuserve.com/internet/iel
http://www.computers.com/reviews/feat
http://www.computers.com/reviews/justi
http://www.computers.com/reviews/justi
http://www.computerstep.com
http://www.corel.com
http://www.corel.com/cgi-bin/redir.exe?
http://www.corel.com/cgi-bin/redir.exe?

If you don't want Internet Explorer to complete your addresses, turn this feature off under Tools>Internet Options>Content> AutoComplete.

3 If you have turned off the Address bar, select Open from the File menu or press Ctrl+O. Both actions bring up the Open dialogue box. Type an address, or select one from the drop-down list, and click OK.

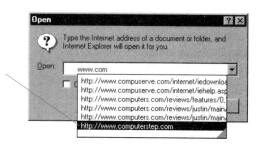

Problems you may have

The Internet is constantly evolving: sites come and go and servers are moved or upgraded. It's also subject to its fair share of bugs and bad connections, so sometimes Internet Explorer will give you an error message instead of displaying the page you want to see:

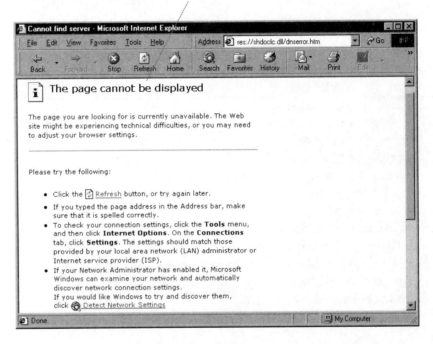

Although Internet Explorer gives you a long list of possible causes and solutions, the vast majority of errors arise because:

I   You've typed the address incorrectly. Try again, checking the address carefully before you click Go or press Enter.

2   The computer where the page is stored is temporarily out of action. Try again in a few hours' time.

3   The page you want has moved. Internet Explorer will display the address of the main page of the site; click it and try to find the page from there.

Using links

If you could only get to Web pages by typing in their URLs, browsing the Web would be time-consuming and tedious. Fortunately there's a much easier way to get from page to page: links.

Almost every Web page is linked to anything from one to a hundred or more other pages. Links are usually indicated by coloured, underlined text, and you move to the linked page by clicking this text. For example:

Links can also take you to another section of the same page. For example, many long pages have a list of the major subheadings at the top. Clicking on a heading takes you to the relevant subsection.

Here's a page from the Yahoo! Web directory (see page 68). If you click the blue, underlined text that says 'Reference'...

2 ...you are taken to this page, which lists all the Reference subcategories. Choose a topic and click again to go to another page.

You can tell when the mouse pointer is over a link, because it changes into a pointing hand (🖑). While you're pointing, check the Status bar. You should see the name of the file or site at the other end of the link. The linked text usually changes colour after you've clicked it, so you can see where you've been.

Images can also be used as links – see page 38.

Retracing your steps

Although people often talk about the 'information superhighway', browsing the Web is more like exploring the back streets of a market town: there are lots of directions to head in and it's easy to get lost. However, it's equally easy to retrace your steps.

1 To return to the page you just left, click the Back button or press Alt+Left Arrow.

You can use the History bar to return to any page you've visited in the last two or three weeks – see page 63.

2 To go back several pages, click the arrow to the right of the Back button. Select the page you want to revisit from the pop-up list.

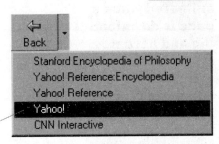

3 Once you've gone back a few pages, you may want to go forward again. Click the Forward button or press Alt+Right Arrow. If you want to go forward several pages, click the arrow to the right of the Forward button.

4 If you get completely lost, you can start again by clicking the Home button or pressing Alt+Home. This takes you to your home page – the page Internet Explorer looks for each time you run it. It's usually a page from your service provider's Web site, or a Microsoft page, but you can change it to anything you like – see page 57.

Stop and Refresh

If the Internet is busy, Web pages can take a long time to arrive, so Internet Explorer enables you to end tedious downloads. You can then go somewhere else, or hope for a better connection and try again.

 The logo in the top right corner is animated when a page is downloading and becomes static when the transfer is complete. You can click on links as soon as you see the text, though – you don't have to wait for the rest of the page to arrive.

1   To abort a download, click the Stop button, select View>Stop or press Esc. Internet Explorer gives up fetching the page.

2   If you change your mind and want to see the rest of a half-downloaded page, click the Refresh button, select View>Refresh or press F5 to reload the page. You should also click Refresh if you think Internet Explorer isn't displaying a page correctly.

3   You can use Refresh to make sure you're seeing the very latest version of a page. For example, pages showing sports results may be updated every few minutes, but the new data won't necessarily be sent to your computer. Sites that work this way usually tell you to 'reload often'.

Understanding Web pages

Web pages start out as unformatted text files – the type of file your word processor produces when you save a document as 'text' or 'plain text'. The designer then specifies how the page should look by inserting pairs of 'tags'. To emphasise a phrase by displaying it in bold type, for example, they insert a 'bold on' tag at the beginning and a 'bold off' tag at the end. When you download the file, Internet Explorer reads the tags and adds the formatting.

 To see what an HTML file 'really' looks like, open a Web page and select View>Source. Internet Explorer transfers the file to Notepad, which displays the tags (look for things in angle <> brackets) as well as the text.

This system is known as HyperText Mark-up Language (HTML). As well as enabling Web designers to format their pages, it makes it possible to include references to other files. For example, links are created using a pair of tags that say, 'If someone clicks anywhere between here (link on) and here (link off), load file xyz.' It might not sound very exciting, but without the ability to include these instructions in the pages, the whole thing would fall apart. You'd have to know the location of every single page instead of just jumping from one to the next.

Tags can also be used to tell the browser to download additional files and insert them into the text. This is how the images arrive: Internet Explorer reads the HTML file, finds an instruction that tells it to 'insert image abc', fetches the image file, works out how everything should look and displays the page. This is why the text often appears first: until you download the HTML file, Internet Explorer doesn't even know there should be pictures.

Unless you want to create your own Web pages, you don't need to worry about the ins and outs of HTML. However, it's worth remembering that the pictures are stored separately from the text, as are sounds, video clips and other additional material.

Images

Before the Web was invented, the Internet was a text-based medium. You could access lots of useful information from all around the globe, and many interesting discussions were held. Unfortunately it all looked about as exciting as pages from the phone book, so no-one wanted to put the Internet on television.

The addition of images changed all that. They make the Web colourful and interesting, add personality and give it a friendly face. However, they aren't just there to make the pages pretty; they can also help you get from one to the next. The four most common types of image link are:

If you see an icon with a red cross (☒) where an image should be, Internet Explorer either can't find or can't display the image file.

1   *Buttons* – many Web sites use icons and toolbars to help you navigate. For example, the Yahoo! Web directory (see page 68) has buttons that take you to special sections of the site. Clicking the Yahoo! logo takes you to the main page.

2   *Text* – when Web designers want to use a special font, create fancy text effects or combine text with graphics, they have to save the text in an image file. The result doesn't look like regular linked text, but it functions the same way. For example, the *.net* Web site (see page 67) uses images to create a distinctive menu strip featuring the same fonts as the magazine.

3   *Image maps* – some images contain more than one link. For example, this picture from the *Tomorrow's World* section of the BBC's Web site (see page 77), is linked to Web pages for the five presenters. When you click a person, you're taken to their page. It's called an image map because different parts of the image are 'mapped' to different Web-site addresses.

4   *Thumbnails* – because large images take a long time to download, Web designers often show you a small preview version first. For example, when you search NASA's Gallery (see page 92), you get a page like this. Once you've found the right thumbnail, click it to see a full-size version of the image.

You can find out whether an image is a link by moving the mouse pointer over it. If it changes to a pointing hand, just as it does over a text link (see page 34), clicking will take you to another page.

Sounds and videos

Some Web sites have background music that plays automatically when you download a page. If a tune is getting on your nerves, click Stop to halt the playback.

Sound files can be quite large, and video files are usually enormous. They take a long time to download.

It's more common for sound and video files to be linked to the page, so you can decide whether you want to play them. You'll come across clips in many different formats, but for the moment let's assume you've found a sound file in Windows (filename ends in .wav), basic audio (.au or .snd) or MP3 (.mp3) format, or a movie in Video for Windows (.avi) or MPEG (.mpg or .mpeg) format.

1 To play a sound or video clip, such as these *Tomorrow's World* themes from the BBC's Web site, click the link that leads to the file.

Music

Marvellous music clips of Tomorrow's World past. Download the clips, and relive those years gone by...

The original 1965 Dankworth number
The one with the brain
Starts quiet, rises to a fanfare crescendo
The drums
Last year's baby theme

Windows Media Player tries to play Windows sounds and MPEG videos as they download. This doesn't work very well – you get a few notes or frames, then a pause, then a few more. Just ignore it – you'll be able to play the clip properly when the download is complete.

2 Windows Media Player runs automatically and starts downloading the clip. You'll have to wait while the file is copied on to your hard disk.

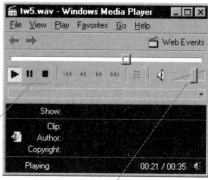

3 When the download is complete, use the tapedeck-style controls to play the sound or video.

4 Use the slider to adjust the volume.

If you come across a clip in a more exotic format, try clicking the link anyway – Windows Media Player may be able to play it. You'll find more information about Internet sound and video in Chapters 5 and 6.

Downloading program files

You can download lots of software from the Internet, including public domain and shareware programs, demo versions of commercial software and add-ons for many programs. Internet Explorer enables you to fetch and run these files in a single operation, but you'll almost always want to save them on to your hard disk instead. You can then experiment with your new software once you've disconnected from the Internet.

1   To download a program file, such as this add-on from *The New York Times* (see page 74), click the appropriate link.

Installing The New York Times Explorer Bar

1. Run this small setup program to install the Explorer bar on your computer.
2. Close all Internet Explorer windows.
3. Restart Internet Explorer.
4. To make the bar appear, click the "View" menu, point to "Explorer Bar", and then click "New York Times on the Web Explorer Bar".

 There's always a chance that a downloaded program might contain a virus. See page 129 for more information.

2   Internet Explorer asks whether you want to open (run) the file or save it on to your hard disk. Choose 'Save this file to disk' and click OK.

3   The standard Save As dialogue box appears. Select a folder and click the Save button.

4   The file is downloaded on to your hard disk – this often takes several minutes. You can continue browsing or switch to another application and carry on working.

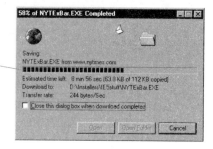

5   Once the download is complete, you have three options. Click Open to run the program straight away.

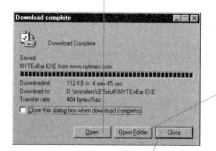

6   Or, click Open Folder to find the file on your hard disk.

7   Or, click Close to close the dialogue box and go on with something else. Don't forget to go back and deal with your new program later!

Compressed files

Web designers often use compression programs to 'archive' the program files linked to their pages. Creating an archive packs everything – setup utility, documentation, help files and the program itself – into a single, neat package. The archive is usually substantially smaller than the original group of files, so it downloads more quickly.

 You'll also come across self-extracting archives. These have an .exe extension and unzip themselves automatically when you run them.

The most popular compression program on the PC, PKZIP, produces archives with a .zip extension. Follow the instructions on the previous page to save them on to your hard disk.

Once you have downloaded a .zip file, you'll need to decompress or 'unzip' it. There are numerous shareware unzippers – try PKZIP for Windows or WinZip. You can get a copy of PKZIP from PKWARE's Web site at: http://www.pkware.com/

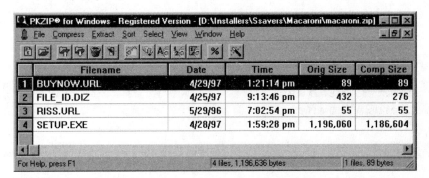

WinZip is available from Niko Mak Computing at: http://www.winzip.com/

Other types of archive you may encounter include .hqx, .sit, .sea (Macintosh), .gz, .Z, .tar and .gtar (Unix) files. It's unlikely you'll be able to make use of the contents of these files, so it's best to avoid them.

Saving Web pages

Don't forget that material on the Web is protected by copyright. Keeping copies for personal reference is unlikely to get you into trouble, but you mustn't reuse or redistribute text, images, sounds or videos without permission.

Sometimes you'll come across a Web page with lots of useful information that you might want to refer to in the future. Saving it on to your hard disk enables you to reload it whenever you want, without the expense of logging on and downloading it again.

| To save a Web page, pull down the File menu and select Save As. This brings up the standard Save As dialogue box.

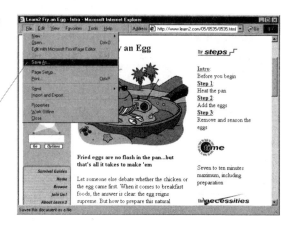

See page 90 for more about the Learn2 Web site.

2 Choose a folder and give the file a name.

3 Select 'Web Page, complete' to save the text and the pictures as separate files.

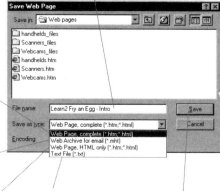

4 Or, select 'Web Archive for email' to save the text and the pictures as a single document.

6 Or, select 'Text File' to just save the text, without formatting.

5 Or, select 'Web Page, HTML only' to save the text and the formatting instructions.

7 Click Save to finish.

...cont'd

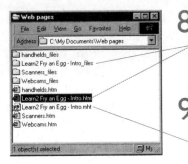

8 'Web Page, complete' produces a .htm file for the page and a folder full of picture files.

9 'Web Archive for email' produces a single file with an .mht extension.

10 Either way, you can load the page back into Internet Explorer by double-clicking on the file. Alternatively, select Open from Internet Explorer's File menu. Click the Browse button to find the file.

Saving individual files
You can also save images, sounds and videos.

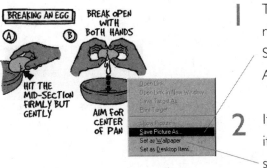

1 To save an image, right-click it and select Save Picture As from the menu.

2 If you want to display it on your desktop, select Set as Wallpaper instead.

3 The easiest way to save a sound or video file is by right-clicking the link that leads to it. Select Save Target As from the pop-up menu.

Printing Web pages

If you're gathering information for a report or project, printing Web pages is sometimes more convenient than saving them. You don't end up with a hard disk full of Web pages, and you can scribble notes in the margins or highlight important passages. You can also print a table showing all the Web pages linked to the current one.

You can also print a page by clicking the Print button, but you'll bypass the Print dialogue and won't be able to change any of the options.

1   To print the current page, select File>Print or press Ctrl+P.

2   If the page has frames (see page 103), you need to specify how they should be handled.

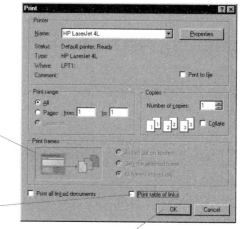

3   To include details of any linked Web pages, select 'Print table of links'.

4   Click the OK button to print the page.

Getting help

Internet Explorer has a Web-style Help file that's handy if you need to check something while you're on-line.

The Contents section only lists some of the topics. If you're looking for information about a specific feature, it's best to go straight to the Index. Only use the Search section (covered overleaf) if the Index has failed you. It finds more topics, but many of them will only mention your keyword in passing.

1 To open the Help file, go to Help>Contents and Index.

2 Click a chapter title, then select a topic. The text is displayed on the right.

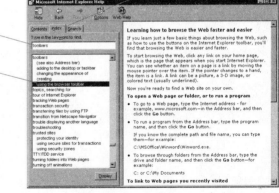

3 Some pages have Web-style links to related material.

4 If you can't find the topic you want, click the Index tab.

5 Type in a keyword.

6 The relevant section of the index appears. Double-click a topic to display it on the right.

...cont'd

 You can access the Support section of Microsoft's Web site by selecting Help>Online Support. However, most of the information you'll find there is aimed at expert users.

7 Still need more information? Click the Search tab.

8 Enter your keyword again.

9 Click the List Topics button.

10 This time you see all the topics that mention your keyword. Double-click one to read the text.

Finding your way

There are over 100 million Web pages and it's easy to lose your way as you jump from one to the next. This chapter explains how to use Favorites, Shortcuts and the Links bar to keep track of the ones you visit regularly. It also shows you how to find information on the Web.

Chapter Three

Covers

Creating Favorites

As you explore the Web, you'll often come across sites you may want to visit again in the future. Rather than writing down the address, add the site to Internet Explorer's Favorites menu.

 You can also right-click on the page and select Add to Favorites from the pop-up menu. Right-click on a link to create a Favorite for the page at the other end.

1 To create a Favorite for the current page, select Add to Favorites from the Favorites menu.

 The 'Make available offline' option is covered in Chapter 8.

2 Check the name – you may need to change it to something shorter or clearer. Click OK to create the Favorite.

 See page 76 to find out more about the Internet Movie Database.

3 You can return to this page whenever you want, simply by selecting it from the Favorites menu.

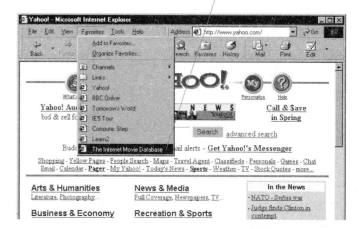

Managing Favorites

Once you have 15–20 Favorites, you'll need to start organising them into folders. This creates submenus and makes it easier to find the one you want.

1   Select Organize Favorites from the Favorites menu.

2   Click the Create Folder button.

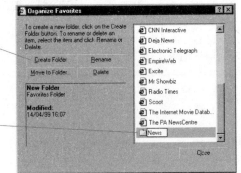

3   Type in a name for your new folder and press Enter.

 You will already have a Links folder – see page 56. You may also have a Channels folder. Channels were a feature of Internet Explorer 4. They're still supported in version 5, but they really aren't worth bothering with.

4   Select a Favorite that needs to be relocated into the new folder. Internet Explorer displays some information about it.

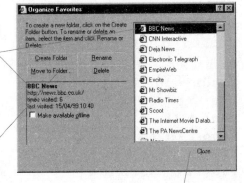

5   Click Move to Folder.

You can also drag Favorites to the correct folders.

6   Select the folder and click OK.

7   Click Close to finish organising your Favorites.

To save a new Favorite straight into a folder, click the Create in>> button (see step 2 on page 50). Select the correct folder, then click OK.

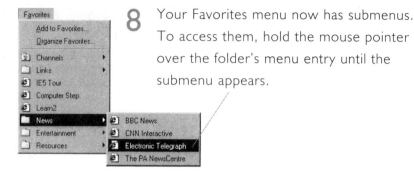

8 Your Favorites menu now has submenus. To access them, hold the mouse pointer over the folder's menu entry until the submenu appears.

Managing Favorites with Windows Explorer

All your Favorites are stored on your hard disk, each in its own file, in the C:\Windows\Favorites folder. You can view them using Windows Explorer. Once you have a lot of Favorites, you may find it easier to organise them using this program, which lets you drag them around in groups.

 Want to back up all your Favorites? Go back to Internet Explorer and select File>Import and Export. The Import/ Export Wizard will help you export all your Favorites into a single file. Copy this file on to a floppy disk for safekeeping.

1 Run Windows Explorer and click your way to the Favorites folder.

2 Use File>New>Folder to create any new folders you require.

3 Select your Favorites, holding down Shift or Ctrl to select several at once, and drag them to the correct folder.

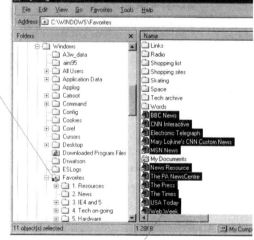

Favorites bar

The Favorites bar gives you another way to access your Favorites. It's more convenient than the menu, but takes up quite a lot of the main window.

If you switch to Full Screen mode (see page 29), you'll see a push-pin ( ) icon at the top of the Favorites bar. When it's on its side, the Favorites bar slides in and out from the left-hand side of the screen. Click the pin into the 'stuck into the page' position ( ) to make the bar stay in one place.

I Click the Favorites button to open the Favorites bar.

2 Click a folder to see a list of Favorites. A second click closes the folder.

3 Click a Favorite to open a Web page (in this case, the BBC's News site – see page 73).

4 Use the scroll bar to move up and down the list.

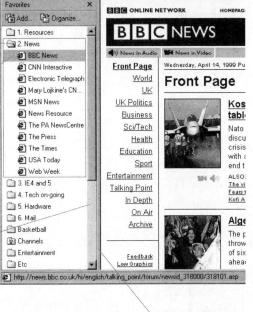

5 Drag the divider left or right to change the size of the bar.

6 Click the Favorites button again to close the Favorites bar. You can also click the cross ( ) in the top right corner.

...cont'd

Managing Favorites with the Favorites bar

You can use the Favorites bar to reorganise your Favorites.
It enables you to move, delete and rename both Favorites
and folders. You can also change their order.

1   Click Add to create a Favorite for the page you're currently
viewing (see page 50).

2   Click Organize to open the
Organize Favorites dialogue
box (see page 51).

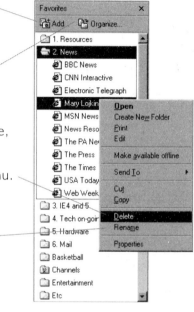

3   To delete a folder or Favorite,
right-click on it and select
Delete from the pop-up menu.

4   To change its name, select
Rename instead.

**You can
use all
these
tricks in
the Favorites menu,
too. There's even an
extra option: when
you right-click on a
folder or Favorite,
you can choose
'Sort by Name' to
sort that section
of the menu into
alphabetical order.**

5   To move a folder or Favourite, point to
it with the mouse, then press and hold
the left button.

6   Drag the selected item to a new
location. You can move it to a particular
position in the list by looking out for the
black divider that appears when the
mouse pointer is between two items.

54

Internet Shortcuts

An Internet Shortcut is a Favorite that lives on your Desktop, rather than in the Favorites menu. Double-clicking on it runs Internet Explorer, connects you to the Internet and takes you to the specified page.

Internet Shortcuts are useful for sites you visit frequently. For example, you could use a Shortcut to the BBC's News site (see page 73) to start Internet Explorer first thing in the morning. Later in the day you might want to use a search engine or go straight to a sports or entertainment site.

 If you can see some of your Desktop alongside Internet Explorer's window, you can also make Shortcuts using the page icon (⊠) at the left-hand end of the Address bar. Drag it on to your desktop to make a Shortcut for the current page.

1 To create an Internet Shortcut, right-click on the background of the Web page and select Create Shortcut from the pop-up menu. Alternatively, go to File>Send>Shortcut To Desktop.

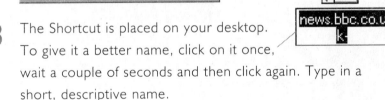

2 A dialogue box appears. Click OK to confirm the creation of the Shortcut.

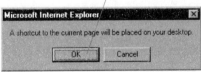

3 The Shortcut is placed on your desktop. To give it a better name, click on it once, wait a couple of seconds and then click again. Type in a short, descriptive name.

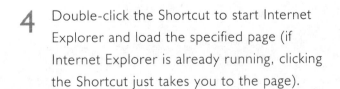

4 Double-click the Shortcut to start Internet Explorer and load the specified page (if Internet Explorer is already running, clicking the Shortcut just takes you to the page).

Links bar

The Links bar provides another way to access your favourite sites. When you install Internet Explorer, it contains buttons for sites selected by Microsoft or your service provider. You can replace these with your own top choices.

1 If you don't find the default links useful, right-click them and select Delete from the pop-up menu.

There are several ways to create new buttons.

You can also make a Links bar button for the current page by dragging the page icon (🖻) from the Address bar to the Links bar.

2 To add the page you're currently viewing, select Add to Favorites from the Favorites menu. Click Create in>> and select the Links folder.

3 Another option is to open the Favourites bar and drag a few of your Favorites on to the Links bar. You need to place them alongside the existing buttons – a black divider appears when the mouse is in the right place.

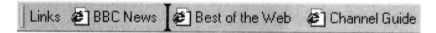

4 You can also select a link on a Web page and add the page at the other end to the Links bar. Point to the link, hold down the right mouse button and drag it onto the bar.

5 If you add more sites than Internet Explorer can display, two arrows appear at the right-hand end of the bar. Click them to see the rest of the buttons in a list.

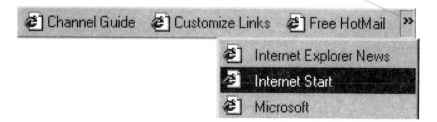

Home Page

 The term 'home page' has several meanings. It can also refer to a personal Web page or the main page of a Web site.

The Home Page is the page Internet Explorer looks for each time you run it. You're also taken to this page when you click the Home button or press Alt+Home.

The default Home Page is usually one of your service provider's Web pages, although you may be taken to the Internet Start Page on Microsoft's Web site instead. You don't have to stick with the default setting, though – you can change the Home Page to any page you visit often or find useful, such as a news site or Web directory.

 If you know the URL, you can just type it into the Address box.

1 To change your Home Page, browse to the site you'd like to use. Select Tools>Internet Options and click the General tab.

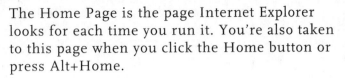

2 Click Use Current to change your Home Page.

3 Or, click Use Default to revert to the Home Page that was specified when you installed Internet Explorer.

4 Or, click Use Blank if you often want to run Internet Explorer without connecting to the Internet. It will load a blank page from your hard disk instead of running the connection software.

Searching the Internet

Browsing aimlessly around the Internet is easy – you just keep clicking links until you come across something interesting. More often than not, though, you'll be looking for specific information. If you were in a library, you'd consult the catalogue; on the Internet, you turn to the organisations and individuals who devote their time to indexing the World Wide Web.

There are three basic types of index. Directories list sites by topic and subtopic, enabling you to focus in on the area of interest gradually. If you are looking for an explanation of Albert Einstein's Theory of Relativity, for example, you select Science, and then Physics, Relativity and so on. Web directories work well when you're researching a broad area.

 In addition to search engines that cover the entire Web, you'll encounter more specialised ones that concentrate on particular topics or sites. The technology is the same; they just use a smaller database.

If you're looking for something more specific, you're better off using a search engine. Search engines enable you to search or 'query' a vast database that indexes all the text on millions of Web pages. You simply type in a few keywords – 'Albert', 'Einstein' and 'relativity', perhaps – and the site returns a list of all the Web pages where they appear. In most cases you get a brief extract that helps you work out which pages are relevant.

Search engines are thorough but not very bright. They'll often return thousands or tens of thousands of 'hits', all of which contain your keywords, but few of which answer your question. If you choose your keywords carefully, though (see page 62), they can be very efficient.

The third type of index is a meta-list – a page of links dedicated to a particular subject, sometimes with brief descriptions of each site. Meta-lists are usually prepared by people who've spent a lot of time tracking down useful sites and want to share the results.

A search may take you through all three types of index. A Web directory might point you to a meta-list, which might recommend a site, which in turn might have a search engine that helps you find the most relevant page.

Search Assistant

Internet Explorer's Search Assistant provides easy access to several search engines. It displays the Search controls down the left-hand side of the screen, enabling you to keep the results in view while you check out individual sites.

1 Click the Search button to open the Search Assistant.

2 Tell the Search Assistant what you're trying to find.

3 Enter your keywords.

4 Click Search.

You can conduct a quick search from the Address bar. Type 'go', 'find' or '?' followed by the word(s) you want to find, then press Enter.

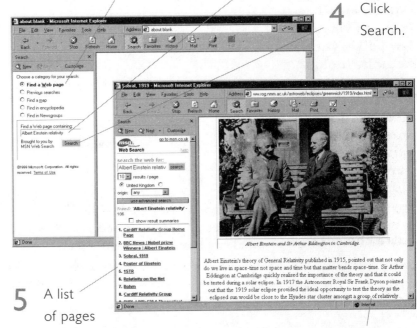

5 A list of pages appears on the left. Hold the mouse over a link for more details.

6 When you click a link, the corresponding page appears on the right.

When you find a good site, go to Tools>Show Related Sites to open another bar that lists sites that have something in common with the current one.

7 If you don't find what you're looking for, click Next to send the keywords to another search engine. Click the arrow next to the Next button to select a specific engine.

...cont'd

8 Click New when you're ready to start another search.

The controls you see when you click the Search button aren't loaded from your hard disk; you're actually looking at a page from Microsoft's Web site. Microsoft sometimes changes this page to add new search engines. Don't be surprised if you open the Assistant and find extra choices.

9 The 'Previous searches' option enables you to go back to keywords you've used in earlier searches.

10 The 'map' option locates places; 'encyclopedia' finds articles in the on-line version of Encarta, Microsoft's multimedia encyclopedia. 'Newsgroups' finds messages posted to Usenet newsgroups – see Chapter 10.

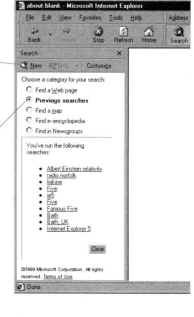

The Search Assistant is convenient, but its range of search engines is quite limited, and it doesn't tell you how to make the most of them. It's a good idea to visit their home pages (see pages 68–70 for some addresses) to find out about any special facilities they offer.

Customising the Search Assistant

You'll probably find that some search engines are more helpful than others, and you may not use some of the Search Assistant's categories. Clear out the dead wood by using the Customize option to fine-tune your choices.

If you don't like the Search Assistant and just want to use your favourite search engine, select 'Use one search service...'

1 Click Customize.

2 Select the categories and search engines you want to use.

3 To move your favourite engine to the top of the list, so it is used first, select it and click the blue 'up' arrow.

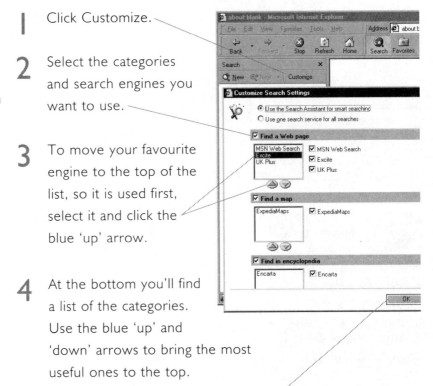

4 At the bottom you'll find a list of the categories. Use the blue 'up' and 'down' arrows to bring the most useful ones to the top.

5 Click OK to finish, or Cancel to go back to Internet Explorer without implementing your changes.

Searching tips

Searching the Internet can be frustrating, but with practice it's possible to locate information quickly and efficiently.

1   Decide whether you're searching or browsing. If you're looking for general information about a broad topic, such as 'relativity', use a directory to find sites that concentrate on that subject. If you're looking for a specific person or event, use a search engine.

2   Visit the search engine's home page and read the instructions. The popular services all have slightly different options, and what works with one won't necessarily work with another. Once you've found an engine you like, stick with it – the others may find a slightly different selection of sites, but you won't usually miss much.

 If you're taken to a long page and can't work out where your keywords appear, select Edit> Find or press Ctrl+F to search the text.

3   Think words, not concepts. Most search engines simply look for documents containing your keywords, so don't try to describe the concept – you'll get better results by thinking of terms that are likely to appear in the text of a relevant Web page.

4   Refine your search with phrases and extra terms. Most engines allow you to specify that two or more words should appear together, or that the documents must contain some words and not others. For example, searching for 'Einstein' finds over 400,000 pages, whereas searching for 'Einstein' plus 'relativity' brings the total down to 400-odd.

5   Use alternatives. Try 'movie' as well as 'film', and don't forget that 'football' is 'soccer' in many parts of the world.

History bar

If there's any chance you might want to return to a page, it's a good idea to make a Favorite or Shortcut for it. However, all isn't lost if you haven't – you can use the History bar to return to any page you've visited in the last couple of weeks.

1 Click the History button to open the History bar.

2 Click the correct day, then find the server where the page resides.

3 When you find the page you want to return to, click the title to load it into the main window.

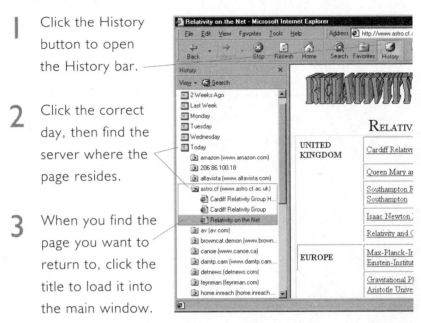

4 If you can't find the page you want to see, click the View button to sort the bar another way.

5 Select By Site if you know where a page was, but can't remember when you last visited it.

6 Or, use By Most Visited to bring your favourite sites to the top of the list.

7 Or, use By Order Visited Today to review today's browsing.

Searching your History

You can hunt through your History for sites that cover a particular subject.

1 Click Search.

2 Enter your keyword.

3 Click Search Now.

4 Relevant pages are listed down the left. Click one to display it on the right.

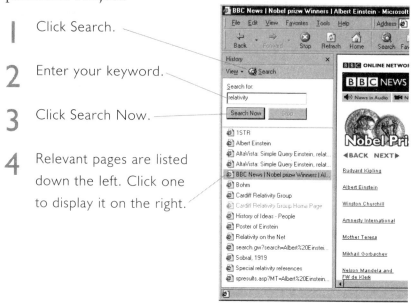

Changing the storage period

You can specify how long the records should be kept. You might want to increase the storage period if you don't log on very often.

1 Go to Tools > Internet Options. Click the General tab.

2 Use the up and down arrows to adjust the number of days information remains in the History folder.

3 Click Clear History if you want to delete your records and start afresh.

4 Click OK to finish.

Exploring the Web

The Internet has so much to offer that it's hard to know where to start. The best way to learn about the Web is by exploring it, so here's a selection of useful, interesting and entertaining sites that provide a good introduction.

Chapter Four

Microsoft

Microsoft

`http://www.microsoft.com/`

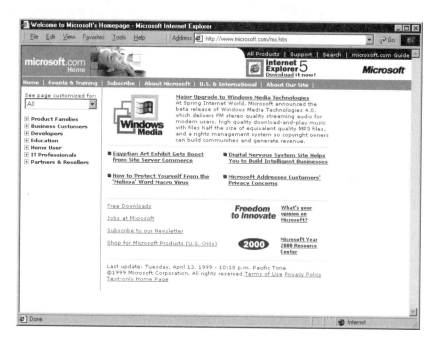

Microsoft's Web site has masses of information about the company's products, including Windows, Word, Excel, the many multimedia CDs and, of course, Internet Explorer. You can download demos and add-ons, learn about new technologies or use the Support section to solve technical problems. The Knowledge Base – a database of solutions and step-by-step guides used by Microsoft's technical-support people – is worth a look if one of your applications is playing up.

A 'mirror' is a copy of a Web site on another server, often in a different part of the world.

There's also a European mirror of Microsoft's site. It's usually less busy than the main site, so pages and files download more quickly. Find it at:

`http://www.eu.microsoft.com/`

There's a UK-specific site at:

`http://www.eu.microsoft.com/uk/`

The Internet

CNET

`http://www.cnet.com/`

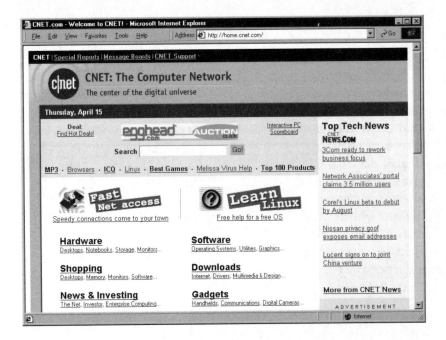

CNET: The Computer Network is an American company that combines television programming and Web sites to provide information about computers, the Internet and future technology. Its Web site offers a beginner-friendly mixture of news, reviews and features, including 'how to' guides and backgrounders that'll help you make sense of the latest technology.

You could also try:

HotWired, the electronic incarnation of *Wired* magazine. Iconoclastic but somewhat impenetrable, it sets trends as well as documenting them. Find it at:

`http://www.hotwired.com/`

For a UK perspective, try the on-line version of *.net* magazine at:

`http://www.netmag.co.uk/`

Directories

Yahoo!

`http://www.yahoo.com/`

Most of the sites featured in this chapter are large, well established and unlikely to move or vanish. If you do find that one of the addresses is no longer valid, you may still be able to find the site using a directory or search engine.

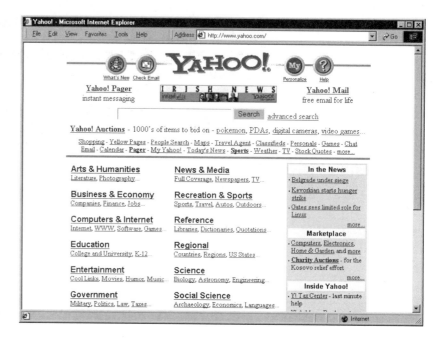

Yahoo! is a hierarchical directory of Web sites and (some) other Internet resources. Each of the 14 categories is progressively subdivided into more tightly defined subcategories, enabling you to work your way down to a list of sites that concentrate on the subject of interest. It's extensively cross-referenced and you can speed things up by searching for keywords.

For further coverage of UK-based Internet sites of interest, see 'Internet Directory UK', also in the 'in easy steps' series.

Yahoo! has several more specialised offshoots, including Yahooligans! for younger browsers, Yahoo! UK & Ireland and the customisable My Yahoo!

You could also try:

UK Plus, a small but friendly Web directory "dedicated to finding and reviewing everything that a UK reader might consider worth seeing on the Internet". Find it at:
`http://www.ukplus.co.uk/`

Search engines

Search engines and directories are some of the most popular sites on the Web. Many offer additional services and the line between directories and search engines has become very indistinct.

AltaVista

`http://www.altavista.com/` or `http://av.com/`

AltaVista enables you to search for Web sites containing a particular word or phrase. It takes some practice to get the best out of it – it's easy to make your search too broad, producing thousands of hits – but it does enable you to find information very quickly. Extras include Babel Fish, a utility that translates French, German, Italian, Portuguese or Spanish Web pages into English, or vice versa.

You could also try:

Lycos, which also indexes pictures and sounds. Find it at:
`http://www.lycos.co.uk/`

Excite, which enables you to refine your search by clicking a 'More like this' link next to entries that hit the mark, at:
`http://www.excite.co.uk/`

Ask Jeeves, which accepts plain-English questions, at:
`http://www.askjeeves.com/`

Specialised search engines

Filez

http://www.filez.com/

The Filez database has details of over 75 million files stored on FTP sites (see page 111), enabling you to find programs, graphics, movies, sounds, icons and so on. You can search by name or, more usefully, description. It's also possible to specify a particular operating system or type of file.

You could also try:

Yahoo! People Search, for e-mail addresses, at:
http://people.yahoo.com/

Deja News, which covers Usenet newsgroups, at:
http://www.dejanews.com/

Scoot, for UK businesses, at:
http://www.scoot.co.uk/

CNET's Search.com has links to over 100 specialist resources. Find it at:
http://www.search.com/

Best and worst

The Web 100
http://www.web100.com/

The Web 100 lists the best sites on the Web, as voted for by Internet users. The list is updated every hour, can be viewed by subject as well as ranking and includes a brief review of each site. Most of the voters are American, so some sites are too US-oriented to hold much interest for British Internet users. However, you'll also find plenty of must-see sites with international appeal.

You could also try:
Cool Site of the Day, for a daily pointer to a Web site considered 'cool', at:
http://cool.infi.net/

Project Cool, for sites that are innovative or beautifully designed. The Sightings section provides a daily link.
http://www.projectcool.com/

The Useless Pages, for a selection of pointless sites, at:
http://www.go2net.com/internet/useless/

Service providers

InetUK

`http://www.limitless.co.uk/inetuk/`

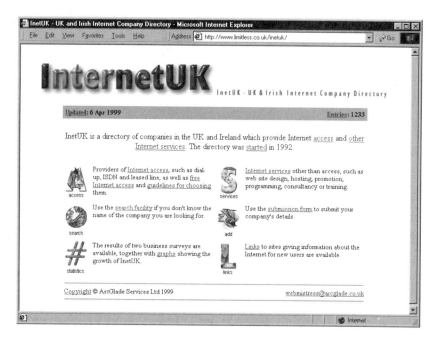

InetUK maintains a list of Internet service providers in the UK and Ireland, with links to their Web sites. Free services are included in the main list, and also in one of their own. It's handy if you're thinking about changing providers.

You could also try:

The Cybercafe Search Engine lists cyber cafés and public Internet access points in over 100 countries. Find it at: `http://www.cybercaptive.com/`

Don't forget to visit your service provider's Web site, which may provide technical support as well as details of its services. The information you were sent when you opened your account should include the site's address.

News

The Electronic Telegraph
http://www.telegraph.co.uk/

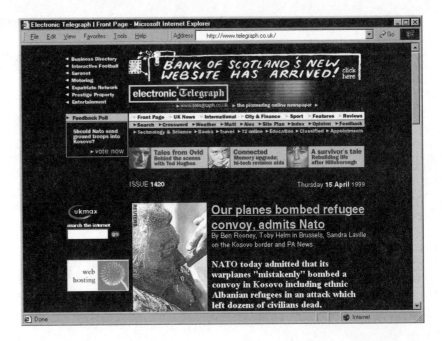

The on-line edition of *The Telegraph* has everything you'd
expect in a printed newspaper, including UK, international
and City news, sport, weather, a crossword, cartoons and
classified ads. Catch up on older stories by searching the
archive, which goes back to November 1994.

You could also try:

BBC News, a typically polished effort with all the headlines
plus audio and video, background articles and 'Talking
Point' areas where you can vote on topical issues. Find it at:
http://news.bbc.co.uk/

The PA News Centre, for headline news from the Press
Association's news agencies, at:
http://www.pa.press.net/

NewsNow, for links to the top stories from over 100 other
news services, at:
http://www.newsnow.co.uk/

CNN Interactive

http://www.cnn.com/

One of the great things about the Internet is the tremendous choice of viewpoints. Rather than sticking to British news sites, for example, you can pop over to the States for an American perspective on US and world news.

CNN's site provides a wide range of clearly presented stories, complete with sound samples and video clips. It's updated throughout the day and there are lots of cross-references and links to other sites.

You could also try:

The New York Times, for in-depth coverage of international and US news. Find it at:

http://www.nyt.com/

News Resource, for links to on-line news services from all around the globe, at:

http://newo.com/news/

Weather

The BBC Weather Centre

`http://www.bbc.co.uk/weather/`

Come rain or shine, the BBC Weather Centre brings you forecasts, weather lore and information about its services. You can meet the team and find out how the 122 daily broadcasts are made, or see how this year's weather is measuring up. The Weather Show section includes a glossary, a temperature convertor and an almanac packed with 'on this day' weather trivia.

You could also try:

The Met Office, for national, regional and marine forecasts and information about weather forecasting, at:
`http://www.meto.govt.uk/`

Entertainment: Movies

The Internet Movie Database
`http://uk.imdb.com/`

The Internet Movie Database contains everything you're likely to want to know about over 180,000 movies. As well as cast lists, synopses, reviews and ratings, it has links to everything from official studio sites to fan pages for directors and actors.

You could also try:

Mr Showbiz, an entertaining celebrity-oriented site that supplements its news and reviews with profiles, interviews, games and polls. Find it at:
`http://www.mrshowbiz.com/`

Most major releases have promotional Web sites with pictures, sound and video clips, games and so on. Use the Internet Movie Database to track them down.

Scoot (see page 70) has a film-finding service that can tell you what's on at your local cinema.

Television

BBC Online
http://www.bbc.co.uk/

BBC Online is the BBC's public-service offering. In addition to news (see page 73) and weather (see page 75), it has information about everything from *TeleTubbies* and *Blue Peter* to *EastEnders, Tomorrow's World* and *WatchDog*. You can also check television and radio schedules and get tickets for BBC shows.

Beeb @ the BBC (http://www.beeb.com/) provides a home for more commercial offerings.

You could also try:
Channel 4, for listings and information, at:
http://www.channel4.com/

Sky Online, for all things satellite-related, at:
http://www.sky.co.uk/

Toaster, for terrestrial, satellite and cable listings, at:
http://www.toaster.co.uk/

Music

dotmusic

http://www.dotmusic.com/

'dotmusic' is a UK e-zine (electronic magazine) with news, general and specialist charts and information about many popular artists. You can listen to some of the top tracks and the Previews section has clips of forthcoming singles.

You could also try:

Jazz Online, which specialises in all styles of jazz music, "from traditional to straight-ahead to progressive to fusion to contemporary and more". Find it at:
http://www.jazzonline.com/

Classical Insites, for information about composers, performers, recordings, genres and historical periods, at:
http://www.classicalinsites.com/

Magazines

Pathfinder
http://www.pathfinder.com/

Many popular magazines have Web sites featuring extracts and additional material.

Time Warner's Pathfinder is home to the on-line editions of *Time, Money, Fortune* and *Entertainment Weekly*. They aren't quite as convenient as real magazines – you can't read them on trains, for example – but they're free, and they come into their own when you want to look back at articles and reviews from previous months.

You could also try:
Condé Nast London, for the on-line versions of *Vogue, GQ, Tatler, Vanity Fair, House and Garden, World of Interiors* and *Condé Nast Traveller*, at:
http://www.condenast.co.uk/

National Geographic, for travel and natural history, at:
http://www.nationalgeographic.com/

E-zines

Salon

`http://www.salon.com/`

The ease and speed with which Web pages can be created has also spawned a host of Web-only magazines or 'e-zines'.

Salon covers arts and entertainment, books, parenting, health, travel and technology. In addition to Sunday supplement-style features, it has interviews, news and media commentary, comic strips and 'table talk' forums. It concentrates on quality writing and is updated daily.

You could also try:

The Onion, a satirical newspaper for over 18s, at:
`http://www.theonion.com/`

Women's Wire, for a female perspective on careers, money, style, entertainment and personal development, at:
`http://www.womenswire.com/`

John Labowitz lists over 3,500 e-zines at:
`http://www.meer.net/~johnl/e-zine-list/`

Internet broadcasts

Broadcast.com

`http://www.broadcast.com/`

Want to listen to a basketball game, or watch NASA TV? Broadcast.com transmits thousands of hours of radio, television and Internet-only shows each week, using streaming audio and video (see page 105). Some programs are archived so you can download them whenever you want; others are only available live. You can also play music via the CD Jukebox or listen to audiobooks.

You could also try:

Pseudo, an interactive Internet television site that enables you to chat with other Net users and people in the studio as you watch the live broadcasts. Find it at:
`http://www.pseudo.com/`

OnNow, for a quick guide to shows that are on now, at:
`http://www.onnow.com/`

Web Events, Microsoft's catalogue of broadcasts, at:
`http://webevents.microsoft.com/`

Chat

Talk City
http://www.talkcity.com/

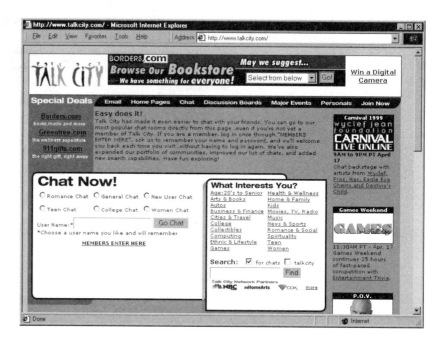

See page 101 for more about chat, and page 110 for an explanation of Java.

Chat sites enable you to communicate with other Internet users in real time. Talk City is one of the best, partly because it uses a Java applet to keep the conversation flowing smoothly, and partly because its strict code of conduct deters troublemakers. You can talk about anything from music and movies to religion and politics, or play one of the fast-paced word games.

You could also try:
WBS, a popular forms-based chat site. It is slower than Talk City, but very easy to use. Find it at:
http://wbs.net/

Sport

Football 365

`http://www.football365.com/`

Football365 is a football site that's updated 365 days a year – hence the name. Its main attraction is a daily newspaper that you can have delivered by e-mail. The Web site also has live scores from the English and Scottish leagues, breaking news, discussion forums and humorous columns.

You could also try:

CricInfo, "the home of cricket on the Internet". It's maintained by enthusiasts and has more statistics than you can shake a bat at. Find it at:
`http://www-uk.cricket.org/`

Golf.com, an extensive site with news, commentary and advice for those who like a good walk spoiled, at:
`http://www.golf.com/`

Formula1.com, an unofficial Formula 1 site with lots of facts and fun, at:
`http://www.formula1.com/`

NBA.com
http://www.nba.com/

Having access to the Internet makes it easy to follow sports that aren't popular in the UK, such as baseball, basketball and American football. You can also get up-to-the-minute results from international events.

The NBA site enhances its news, previews, results and profiles with lots of multimedia extras, including sound samples and videos. You can also e-mail questions to selected players or join on-line chat sessions.

You could also try:
Fastball, for Major League baseball, at:
http://www.fastball.com/

NFL.com, for the National (American) Football League, at:
http://www.nfl.com/

NHL.com, for the National (ice) Hockey League, at:
http://www.nhl.com/

Shopping

Amazon
`http://www.amazon.co.uk/`

See page 135 for advice about using your credit card to buy goods over the Internet.

Amazon is one of the most popular on-line retailers. Its UK branch offers over 1.5 million books, often at discounted prices. When you choose a book, it lists other titles bought by people who also bought the one you've selected. If you start with something you know you like, there's a good chance the links will lead you to something equally good. Many titles have also been reviewed by previous customers.

You can also order from the US branch of Amazon (`http://www.amazon.com/`), which offers over 4.5 million titles. Your books take longer to arrive, but you can purchase titles that haven't been published in the UK.

You could also try:
CD Universe, for cut-price CDs, at:
`http://www.cduniverse.com/`

Black Star, for videos and DVDs, at:
`http://www.blackstar.co.uk/`

Sainsbury's

http://www.sainsburys.co.uk/

Books, CDs and videos will keep the family entertained, but sooner or later they'll get hungry. Save yourself the hassle of driving to the supermarket with Sainsbury's Orderline, which enables you to pick out your groceries from an on-line catalogue, then have them delivered to your door. Check the Web site to find out if your area is covered.

You could also try:

Tesco, which also delivers in some areas. Find it at: http://www.tesco.co.uk/

Travel

World Travel Guide
`http://www.travel-guides.com/`

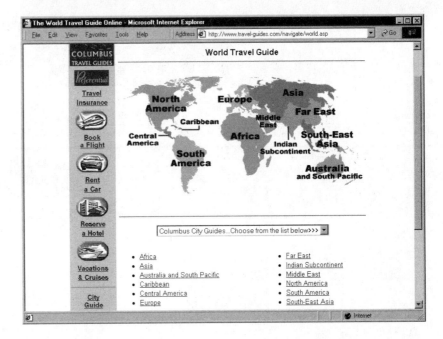

An Internet version of the print publication often used by travel agents, the World Travel Guide is an encyclopaedic reference to every country in the world (including Antarctica). It's short on atmosphere but long on facts, with information about accommodation, climate, essential documents and contact addresses as well as a general overview for each country.

You could also try:
a2btravel, for lots of UK-oriented travel information and on-line booking services, at:
`http://www.a2btravel.com/`

Expedia, Microsoft's travel-booking site, at:
`http://www.expedia.co.uk/`

Lonely Planet On-line, for independent travellers, at:
`http://www.lonelyplanet.com.au/`

Visit Britain
`http://www.visitbritain.com/`

Find out what's worth seeing in the UK with Visit Britain, the British Tourist Authority's Web site. It's relentlessly glowing, but does admit that you might need a waterproof. You can search for activities, events and places to visit or stay, and there's an excellent section on walking.

You could also try:
The RAC, which has an on-line route finder and will e-mail you details of roadworks and traffic jams. Find it at: `http://www.rac.co.uk/`

Railtrack, for train times, at: `http://www.railtrack.co.uk/`

National Express, for bus times and on-line bookings, at: `http://www.nationalexpress.com/`

Multi Media Mapping, for maps of Great Britain, at: `http://uk.multimap.com/`

Reference

Encyclopedia.com
`http://www.encyclopedia.com/`

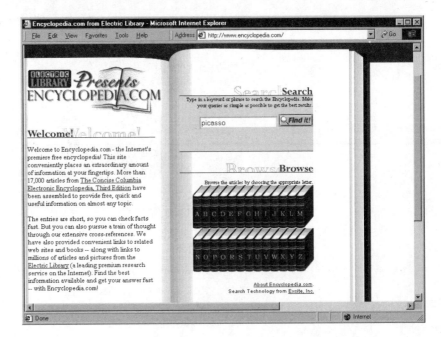

Check your facts by searching articles from the Concise Columbia Electronic Encyclopedia. The company behind it is keen to lure you into the fee-based Electric Library, but the free section should answer most of your questions.

You could also try:
OneLook Dictionaries, which looks for your word in over 450 general and specialist dictionaries. Find it at:
`http://www.onelook.com/`

My Virtual Reference Desk, for pointers to thousands of reference sites, at:
`http://www.refdesk.com/`

Learn2

http://www.learn2.com/

The 'ability utility' offers step-by-step instructions for everything from poaching eggs to fixing broken windows. It's essentially a guide to all the skills everyone is somehow supposed to have acquired, despite the fact that they never made it on to the National Curriculum. Most of the '2torials' deal with domestic matters, but you can also find out how to throw a frisbee, choose a rucksack, clean your computer, get by in French or make paper aeroplanes.

You could also try:

Epicurious Food, for recipes and cooking tips, at: http://food.epicurious.com/

GardenGuides, for help with your plants, at: http://www.gardenguides.com/

BeWell, for health and fitness e-zines and information about common medical conditions, at: http://bewell.com/

Government Information Service

http://www.open.gov.uk/

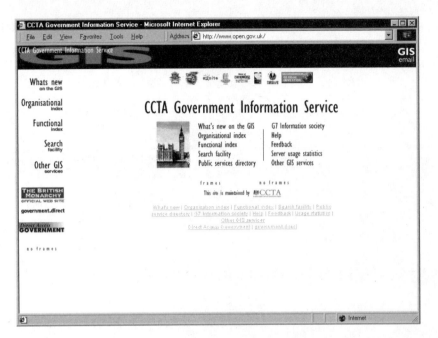

The unattractively named GIS is a gateway to the multitude of UK Government Web sites. From here you can go to the Foreign and Commonwealth Office's site, which has travel advice; or the Inland Revenue Web site, for help with your tax return; or the British Monarchy Web site, for answers to important questions such as, "Is the Queen the wealthiest woman in the world?" Some of the sites are better than others, but there's a tremendous amount of information to be had if you're prepared to dig around. If you're looking for something official, or for any organisation funded by your taxes, the GIS is the place to start.

You could also try:

Want to know how much it costs to send a letter to New Zealand? Ask Royal Mail, at:

http://www.royalmail.co.uk/

Want to check the price of a phone call? Try BT, at:

http://www.bt.com/

Science

NASA

`http://www.nasa.gov/`

The NASA home page is the gateway to a vast collection of information about space and space exploration. Highlights include day-by-day reports from the shuttle, lots of historical information and a 'today@nasa.gov' section with the latest news. It can be hard to work out where your topic might be covered, but few institutions surpass NASA for quantity or quality of publicly available information.

You could also try:

The Why Files, for "the science behind the news", at:
`http://whyfiles.news.wisc.edu/`

Discovery Channel Online, for a wide range of well-presented features, at:
`http://www.discovery.com/`

New Scientist, for news, features, jobs and answers to questions such as, "Why do flying fish fly?" Find it at:
`http://www.newscientist.com/`

Computing: Reference

PC Webopaedia

`http://www.pcwebopaedia.com/`

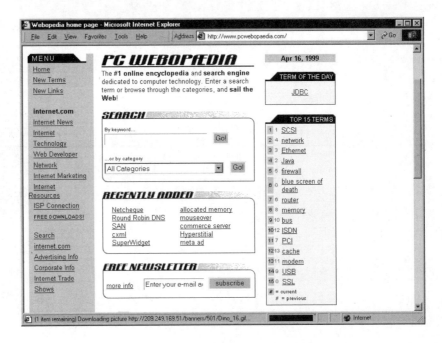

The PC Webopaedia specialises in explaining computer jargon. You can search for terms you've encountered in magazines, or browse through the categories to expand your knowledge. There's even a top 15 list of most requested terms so you can find out what is puzzling other Internet users. Many definitions have links to Web sites where you can get more in-depth coverage.

You could also try:

ZDNet, for reams of information from computer-magazine specialist Ziff-Davis. It isn't as user-friendly as CNET (see page 67), but its reviews tend to be more detailed. Find it at: `http://www.zdnet.com/`

TechWeb, a heavyweight technology news site, at: `http://www.techweb.com/`

Hardware

Gateway 2000

`http://www.gw2k.co.uk/`

Most computer manufacturers have extensive sites that showcase their products, provide technical support and even enable you to buy equipment on-line. They often have a lot more information than you'd find in an advertisement or get from a sales assistant.

Gateway 2000's Web site is no exception: you can examine typical systems, or design your own and order it on-line. The technical support section has solutions to common problems, and you can download the latest driver software.

Also, all the major modem manufacturers have Web sites. Try some of the following for information and advice:

- 3Com/US Robotics   `http://www.3com.co.uk/`
- Diamond   `http://www.diamondmm.co.uk/`
- Hayes   `http://www.hayes.co.uk/`
- Pace   `http://www.pacecom.co.uk/`

Software

Adobe
http://www.adobe.com/

Graphics specialist Adobe has an excellent Web site that provides detailed information about all its products. You can download tryout versions of most programs, or get updates and extras for the ones you already own. The Studio section introduces new techniques, and you can seek inspiration in the gallery.

You could also try:
Corel, creator of CorelDRAW and Corel WordPerfect, at:
http://www.corel.ca/

Use Yahoo! (see page 68) or a search engine to track down other hardware and software companies.

Books

Computer Step

http://www.computerstep.com/

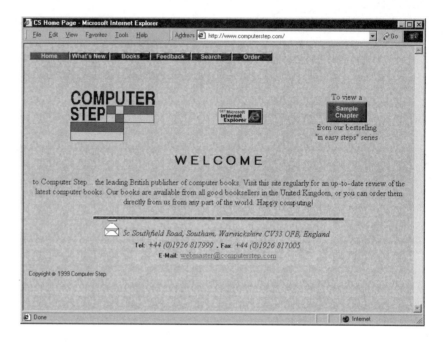

Find out about the other titles in this series from the on-line home of Computer Step, the leading British publisher of computer books.

You could also try:

Computer Manuals, one of Europe's largest mail order retailers of computer books, at:

http://www.compman.co.uk/

Intermediate browsing

This chapter explains some of the tricks Web authors use to make their pages more interesting. You'll learn how to use forms and frames, and find out what is meant by buzz words such as 'streaming', 'Dynamic HTML' and 'Java'. The last two pages covers an older Internet service, FTP, that you may occasionally find useful.

Covers

Forms

Forms enable you to enter keywords into search engines, fill out questionnaires and register for Web sites. They aren't all dry and serious, though – they are also used for interactive gadgets such as automatic letter writers.

Forms are just like dialogue boxes, except the text boxes, drop-down lists, radio buttons and checkboxes are part of a Web page. Once you have filled in the blanks, you click a button to send the data back to the Web server. You'll get a response – another Web page – a few seconds later.

Here's a form from Railtrack's Web site (see page 88):

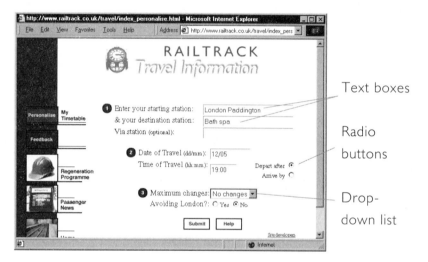

When you fill in your requirements and click Submit, you're given a list of suitable trains.

AutoComplete

Internet Explorer remembers all the things you've typed into forms and tries to anticipate your typing.

Auto-Complete only works when Internet Explorer knows what type of information a box should contain. It won't try to enter your name into an address box.

When you type a 'B' into the Destination box, Internet Explorer lists the 'B' place names you've entered previously. Click the correct one to fill in the box.

> ❶ Enter your starting station: `London Paddington`
> & your destination station: `B`
> Via station (optional):
> | Bath spa |
> | Birmingham New Street |
> | Blackpool |
> | **Brighton** |

You can turn off AutoComplete if you don't find it helpful, or clear the list of words and start again.

1   Select Tools>Internet Options, then click the Content tab. Click the AutoComplete button.

2   Deselect any or all of the AutoComplete options.

3   Click Clear Forms if you want Internet Explorer to forget all the words you've typed into forms.

AutoComplete Settings

AutoComplete lists possible matches from entries you've typed before.

Use AutoComplete for
☑ Web addresses
☑ Forms
☑ User names and passwords on forms
  ☑ Prompt me to save passwords

Clear AutoComplete history
[Clear Forms]   [Clear Passwords]

To clear Web address entries, on the General tab in Internet Options, click Clear History.

[OK]   [Cancel]

You can also delete individual items from the list associated with a particular text box.

To delete an item, perhaps because it's wrongly spelt, highlight it in the drop-down list and press Delete.

> ❶ Enter your starting station: `London Paddington`
> & your destination station: `b`
> Via station (optional):
> | Bath spa |
> | Birmingham New Street |
> | Blackpool |
> | **Bongor Regis** |
> | Brighton |

Site registration

Many of the large commercial sites require you to register for access. Usually the company wants to find out what kind of people use the site so it can sell advertising. While it's hard to get excited about ads on Web pages, they do help fund services such as the Electronic Telegraph (see page 73) that you might otherwise have to pay for. Knowing who you are also enables a site to personalise its service. For example, it may display a list of pages that have been added since the last time you visited.

 Don't use the user name and password supplied by your service provider. Anyone who knows these details can use your Internet account, so keep them secret.

Registration involves filling in a form and selecting a user name and password. It's a good idea to write down all your passwords and keep them somewhere safe, because you'll end up with more than you can possibly remember.

Internet Explorer usually asks if it should remember your password. Whether this is a good idea depends on the nature of the site and the number of people who use your computer. See Chapter 7 for more on passwords and Internet security.

Web chat

Web chat enables you to have a conversation – of sorts – with other Web users. It's more like passing notes in class than talking to someone face to face, though.

Chat pages have a form section, where you enter your message, and a message area, where the most recent comments are displayed. To join in, you type a message and click the Send or Submit button.

Some pages update automatically; others require you to click the Refresh button to see your contribution. More sophisticated sites use Java applets (see page 110) rather than forms, but the basic principles are the same.

With luck, someone responds to your comment, you respond to theirs, someone else joins in... and you have a proper conversation. In practice, though, chat pages can be frustratingly slow and the messages correspondingly banal.

One of the best places to try Web chat is the WBS site (see page 82). It's very popular and you can find someone to chat with at any hour of the day.

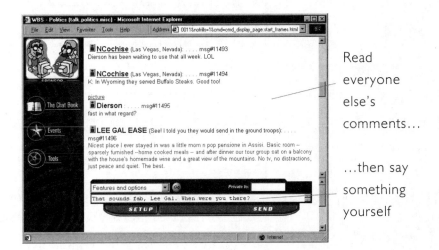

Read everyone else's comments...

...then say something yourself

Message boards

If you enjoy reading and contributing to message boards, you should also investigate Usenet newsgroups – see Chapter 10.

Message boards, sometimes known as forums, are more like the letters page of a newspaper or magazine. Unlike chat sites, they aren't designed for real-time conversation – you just check back periodically to read any new messages, and perhaps add a response. They aren't as immediate as Web chat, but you still see some lively debate.

CNN Interactive (see page 74) has many message boards where you can comment on topical issues.

Once you've read all the messages, scroll to the bottom of the page. Click Post Message to add your own comments.

Frames

Frames divide the main window into two or more 'panes' that can be scrolled or updated separately. They enable Web designers to display several pages at once and are often used to keep a menu within easy reach.

Clicking a link in one of the frames can change its contents, or change the contents of the other frames, or take you to a completely separate Web page. For example, a2btravel's site (see page 87) uses two frames that can be scrolled independently. The menu is always displayed on the left. Clicking a menu item loads the associated page into the right-hand frame.

Most pages that use frames have grey dividing bars between the sections, but it's also possible for the designer to make the divisions almost invisible.

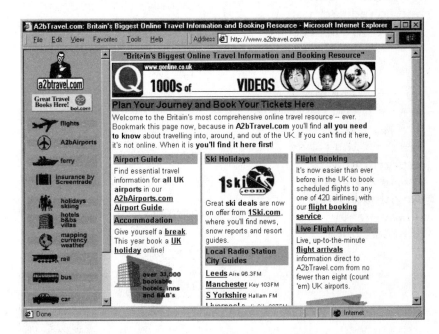

You can print the page as it appears on the screen, or frame by frame.

To print an individual frame, click anywhere within it. Select File> Print and choose the second layout option.

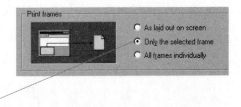

New windows

Web designers can also tell your browser to display a page for a few seconds, then load another one into the same window. This technique is used to create welcome screens, and to redirect you when a site moves.

Clicking on a link sometimes opens a new copy of Internet Explorer instead of simply displaying the page. This isn't a mistake; the designer of the original site is hoping you'll explore the linked page(s), then close the new window and go back to where you were.

You can also choose to open a new window so you can compare two sites, take a detour or keep material on the screen for reference. If the Internet is very busy, you might even want to read a lengthy article in one window while you wait for images to download into another.

1 To open a second window, go to File>New>Window. Initially both windows display the same page, but you can use them independently.

The more you try to do at once, the slower everything gets. Avoid trying to download two image-heavy pages at once.

2 If you're browsing a list of recommended sites, such as this one prepared by the *New Scientist* team (see page 92), you can load them into new windows. Hold down Shift when you click the link, or right-click the link and select Open in New Window from the pop-up menu.

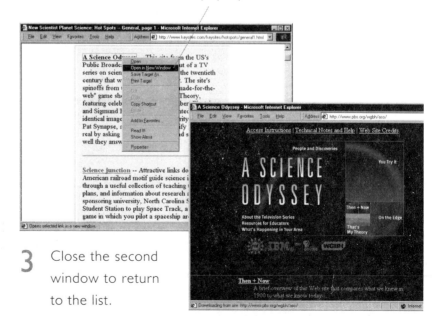

3 Close the second window to return to the list.

Streaming sound and video

Most sound and video files have to be downloaded completely before you play them back (see page 40). This can take a long time – a four-minute song saved in the MP3 format might take 16 minutes to download.

Streaming sound and video formats were invented to overcome this problem. They are compressed so that each minute of sound or video takes a minute to download. This means you can play the 'stream' as it downloads, rather than afterwards.

Streaming formats can't compete with traditional sound and video files for audio and image quality, because a lot of data has to be stripped out to keep downloading and playback in sync. However, you get to see or hear something seconds after you click on a link.

Streaming formats are used to transmit radio and television shows over the Internet, and for live 'Webcasts' of special events. They can also be used for prerecorded material. For example, CD merchants such as CD Universe (see page 85) often let you listen to sample tracks so you can make sure you're buying the right disc.

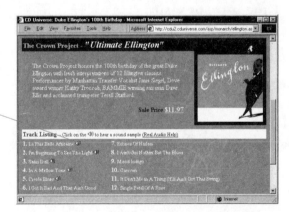

The most common streaming formats are RealAudio (filename ends in .ra or .ram), RealVideo (.rv) and Microsoft's Active Streaming Format (.asf), which is often referred to as Windows Media format. Windows Media Player can in theory handle all three types, but in practice you may need to use RealPlayer (see page 119) for RealAudio and RealVideo files.

... cont'd

Playing streaming sounds and videos

1 To play a file in a streaming format, such as this broadcast from the BBC's World Service (see page 77), click the link that leads to it. There'll be a short pause while Windows Media Player downloads the first few seconds of sound or video, and then it'll start playing automatically.

DISCOVERY 25'/wk.

Exploring the "cutting edge" of science in depth, but at a level accessible to the general listener. A chance to find out more about the discoveries that are likely to have a major impact on society.

◆» Listen to the latest edition of Discovery live in Real Audio -

Click the Web Events button on Windows Media Player's toolbar to find a broadcast to tune into, or visit some of the sites listed on page 81.

2 Use the playback controls to stop, pause and restart the clip. If you are listening to a live broadcast, you can only click Play and Stop. Use the slider to adjust the volume.

3 The player tries to keep a few seconds of sound or video in reserve, in case there are any problems with your connection. Occasionally it'll run out and there'll be a pause in the playback.

4 If your connection is too slow for Windows Media Player to play a live broadcast properly, the smiling sun ( ) changes to sun and cloud ( ), cloud ( ) and rain ( ). You'll notice the broadcast quality deteriorating.

Radio toolbar

The Radio bar is a neat new feature introduced in Internet Explorer 5. It makes it easy to tune in to radio stations that broadcast over the Internet.

To display the Radio toolbar all the time, go to Tools> Internet Options> Advanced. You'll find an 'Always show Internet Explorer Radio bar' checkbox in the Multimedia section of the list.

1 To display the Radio toolbar, right-click on an empty section of any toolbar and select it from the pop-up list.

2 Click Radio Stations and select Radio Station Guide.

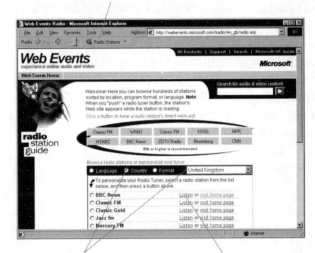

3 Use the radio buttons to sort the list by language, country and format, then pick a subcategory from the drop-down list.

4 Pick a station and click Listen.

5 Listen and enjoy! Use the slider to adjust the volume, or click Stop to turn off your Internet radio.

Interactive Web pages

Because Web pages are displayed on a computer screen, rather than on paper, they can be designed to respond to your input. There are two ways to do this: the designer can add some extra instructions to the HTML document that describes the page, or incorporate a program that runs in a 'hole' in the page. Either way, your computer knows what to do when you point, click or type, so it isn't forever fetching new material from the Web server. This speeds things up and makes browsing more fun.

It's possible for a malicious programmer to use scripts to access private information or cause problems on your computer – see page 133 for more on this and similar hazards.

JavaScript and VBScript

Scripts are sets of instructions that are included in the Web page. You don't see them on the screen, but they tell Internet Explorer what to do when you click a button or enter some text. Scripts are used to display dialogue boxes, carry out simple calculations and add special effects such as scrolling messages. It's even possible to produce simple games and utilities.

The most popular scripting language is Netscape's JavaScript. Microsoft also uses its own language, Visual Basic Script (VBScript). From a Web user's point of view, there isn't much difference between them, and standard installations of Internet Explorer support both languages.

There's nothing you can do about script errors except e-mail the designer of the site with details of the problem.

You're most likely to notice scripts when something goes wrong. If Internet Explorer encounters an instruction it doesn't understand, it displays an error message at the left-hand end of the Status bar.

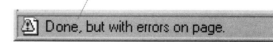

Done, but with errors on page.

You can double-click the icon for a more detailed message, but it won't make much sense unless you're a programmer. Sometimes you can just ignore the error – you may be able to get all the information you want from the page, even though it isn't being displayed properly. However, if there are interactive elements, such as a form to fill out, you'll probably find they don't work properly.

Dynamic HTML

Dynamic HTML is a relatively new technology that was first introduced in Internet Explorer 4, and is supported in Internet Explorer 5. It enables Web authors to create more exciting pages that change as you browse.

Regular HTML enables authors to format their Web pages (see page 37). Dynamic HTML uses scripting to add an interactive element – the formatting can change at a specified time, or in response to your mouse movements, clicks and keystrokes. Items can appear or disappear, move around, change colour and so on. Previously the only way to change the design of a page was to load another one; now the same page can be displayed several different ways. Because you don't have to sit through another download, the changes are almost instantaneous.

Other features of Dynamic HTML include the ability to position images and other objects precisely. They can also be overlapped, made transparent or moved around to animate the page. Pages that display data can include controls that enable you to sort, filter and otherwise manipulate the figures – without any further downloads. Again, this makes browsing faster and more interactive.

The downside of Dynamic HTML is that it's more difficult to work with than the regular sort, so you're more likely to encounter pages with errors. As with most new Web technologies, it's also browser-specific. People with other browsers, or older versions of Internet Explorer, won't see all the features of a dynamic page.

You don't have to do anything special to experience effects created with Dynamic HTML. The capability is built into Internet Explorer, so you'll see them automatically.

To see Dynamic HTML in action, visit the DHTML Zone (`http://www.dhtmlzone.com/`). The Spotlight section has links to innovative Web sites that use DHTML to create interactive pages.

Java

Although they have similar names, Java and JavaScript don't have much in common – they don't even come from the same company.

Java is a programming language developed by Sun Microsystems. It enables Web authors to create small programs, or 'applets', that can be embedded in Web pages. They are downloaded along with the text and images, slotted into the page and run automatically.

The thing that makes Java special – and the reason for all the hype about it – is that a single Java program can run on many different types of computer. It's a two-part system: you have the programs, and you have the Java Virtual Machine, which is built into your browser. The programs are the same for everyone, but the Virtual Machine is specific to a particular type of computer. It acts as an interpreter, converting the standard code into something your computer can understand.

Java is used for animated messages, games and utilities. You'll also come across it on chat sites, where it provides attractive interfaces that permit faster, more fluid conversation than a forms-based approach. Compare the Java-based Talk City site (see page 82) with WBS (see pages 82 and 101) to see how much difference Java can make.

When you download a page with an attached applet, you'll see a blank rectangle, usually grey, in the area the applet uses. After a few seconds, the rectangle is replaced by the animation or game (look out for 'Applet Loaded' and 'Applet Started' messages in the Status bar). You don't have to start or stop the applet; you just watch or play, then move on to another page.

The difference between Java applets and the technologies discussed on the previous two pages is that applets are downloaded separately from the document that describes the page, whereas scripts and Dynamic HTML are part of that document. In practice, though, you don't need to know how an effect was achieved to enjoy browsing the page.

File Transfer Protocol

As well as supporting HTTP (HyperText Transfer Protocol – the system that's used to transfer Web pages from the Internet to your computer), Internet Explorer enables you to use an older technology called FTP (File Transfer Protocol).

As the name suggests, FTP is a way of moving files from one computer to another. FTP sites are simply huge libraries of files, organised much like your hard disk. Internet Explorer shows you one folder (directory) at a time.

HENSA is the Higher Education National Software Archive. The Micros section at `ftp://micros. hensa.ac.uk/` **and** `http://micros. hensa.ac.uk/` **contains a large collection of freeware and shareware software that you can download and use on your computer.**

1 To open an FTP site, type the URL into the Address bar. It should begin with `ftp://` (you may have to add this bit yourself). Press Enter or click Go.

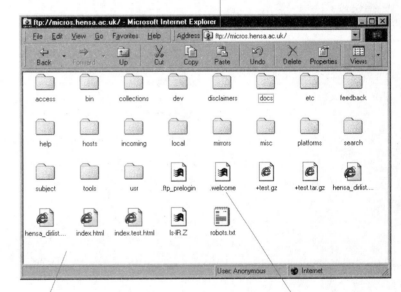

2 Internet Explorer displays a list of folders and files in the main window.

3 Look for welcome, readme or index files to find out how the site is organised. Double-click them to display their contents.

4 Double-click the folder you want to open. To go back to the original one, click the Up button on the Windows Explorer-style toolbar that replaces the Standard buttons.

If you don't see this kind of 'files and folders' display when you log on to an FTP site, you need to install the Internet Explorer Browsing Enhancements component – see page 114.

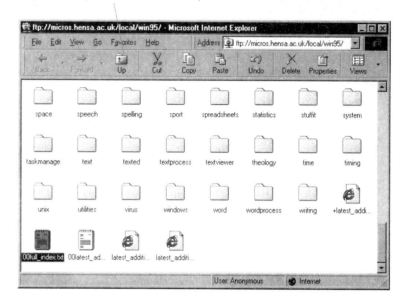

5 When you find an interesting file, double-click on it, then follow the instructions on page 41 to download it on to your hard disk.

Internet Explorer's FTP facilities are useful when a link from a Web site unexpectedly takes you to an FTP site so you can download a file. However, they're very limited compared to those of specialist FTP programs. If you plan to spend a lot of time exploring FTP sites, or have created your own Web site and need to upload it using FTP, get a proper FTP program, such as:

Cute FTP, from GlobalSCAPE at:
http://www.cuteftp.com/

WS_FTP, from Ipswitch at:
http://www.ipswitch.com/

Extending your browser

This chapter explains how to teach Internet Explorer new tricks. It shows you how to update your software and install ActiveX controls and plug-ins, then introduces some of the most popular add-ons.

Chapter Six

Covers

Installing extra components

When you first installed Internet Explorer, you probably didn't install all the extra bits and pieces that come with it. Most people start by selecting the 'Typical installation' option and don't worry about the more obscure components until they've got to grips with the basics.

It's easy to go back and add to your installation if you find you've missed something vital or someone recommends that you try one of the add-on programs.

If you need extra software to view a Web site properly, Internet Explorer will prompt you to install it. Click the Download button to get it straight away.

1 Go to the Start menu and select Settings>Control Panel. Double-click Add/Remove Programs.

2 Select Microsoft Internet Explorer 5 and Internet Tools from the list of programs and click the Add/Remove button.

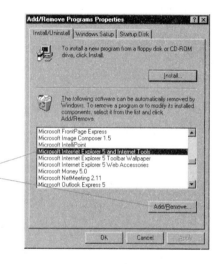

If you got your copy of Internet Explorer from Microsoft's Web site, Add/ Remove assumes you want to download the extra components.

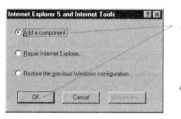

3 Select 'Add a component' and click OK.

4 You'll be prompted to insert your CD.

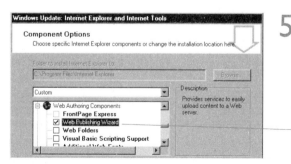

5 The setup program (see page 18) runs again. Select the components you want to install.

Updating your software

When you buy software in a shop, you're buying a finished product. You take it home, open the box, install it and that's that – nothing changes until the next version comes out.

Preview versions of Internet Explorer **are often very unstable and are not recommended for beginners. Wait for the final version, then upgrade it each time an update appears. Updates fix any security problems that have been discovered (see page 133), and the new version usually works a little better.**

Internet Explorer evolves more gradually. Each version is preceded by 'preview' or 'beta' releases that let experienced browsers get a glimpse of the future. Eventually a 'final' version is released, but the story doesn't end there. Microsoft produces updates and extras every few months, so the software on your CD may not be the latest version.

1 To find out whether Microsoft has released new software, go to the Start menu and select Windows Update. When the Web site is displayed, click the Product Updates link.

2 You'll be asked whether Windows Update can check to see what software is installed on your computer. Click Yes.

3 Internet Explorer displays a list of components you can add. Select the ones you want and click the Download button.

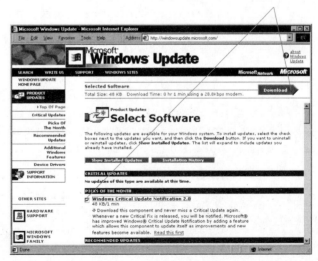

4 Follow the on-screen instructions to download and install the new software. Usually this is a one-step process and you just have to click OK at the end.

Plug-ins and ActiveX Controls

Plug-ins and ActiveX Controls are small pieces of software that add extra features to Internet Explorer. They're often used to handle multimedia files, such as new types of sound and video file or 360-degree panoramas.

You can think of plug-ins and ActiveX Controls as the electronic equivalent of extra blades for your food processor. Each time you want to do something new, you simply download the extra software that enables Internet Explorer to slice, dice, shred and otherwise process the data. Some of the add-ons are produced by Microsoft, but most come from other companies.

Plug-ins are designed to work with Internet Explorer's rival, Netscape Navigator, whereas ActiveX Controls are designed for Internet Explorer. That said, Internet Explorer generally supports both types, and the term 'plug-in' is often used to describe any piece of software that extends your Web browser – including ActiveX Controls.

The main advantage of ActiveX Controls is that they are installed automatically. When you visit a page that requires a new one, Internet Explorer locates and downloads it (see opposite). You get the option to abort the installation, but otherwise everything is done for you, and you shouldn't even have to disconnect from the Internet.

Plug-ins usually have to be installed by hand (see page 118). Once you've checked that the software is compatible with Internet Explorer, you download the version for your operating system, then log off and run the setup program.

Despite the confusing terminology, installing add-ons is actually quite straightforward. If you need an ActiveX Control to view a Web page, Internet Explorer should install it for you. If it doesn't, you probably need to install the software yourself, in which case there'll be a link to a site that you can download it from.

Automatic installation

The great thing about ActiveX Controls is that they are very easy to install. When you encounter a page that requires a new one, Internet Explorer downloads it automatically.

1   Internet Explorer displays a security warning (see page 130) and asks if you want to install the ActiveX Control.

2   Click Yes if you have confidence in the company that published the software, or No to abort the installation.

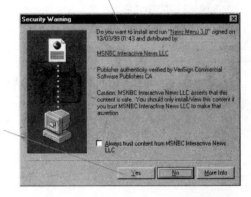

3   If you click Yes, the Control is installed.
    Internet Explorer is able to make use of it straight away, so you'll soon be able to see or hear the additional material.

Manual installation

If you have to install a Control or plug-in manually, you'll usually be directed to the home page of the company that supplies it. For example, sites that use RealAudio (see opposite), normally provide a 'Get RealPlayer' button that takes you to the RealNetworks home page.

It's a good idea to check the system requirements for an add-on before you download it.

1 You'll probably need to enter your details in a form. This enables the Web site to supply the correct version.

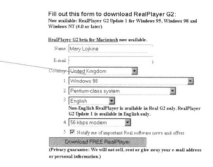

2 Download the file, just as you would any other program file (see page 41). Make sure you know what it's called and where you've put it.

Some of the add-ons described on pages 119–124 are distributed with Internet Explorer, so you won't have to download them all. However, it's worth checking the sites for updates.

3 Once you've disconnected from the Internet, locate the file using Windows Explorer or My Computer. Double-click it to start the setup routine and install the add-on.

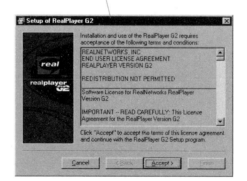

RealPlayer

RealPlayer and Shockwave (see overleaf) are the two most useful plug-ins. They enable you to view some of the most exciting sites on the Web, and they're both very popular.

See page 105 for more on streaming sound and video.

RealPlayer is produced by streaming-sound pioneer RealNetworks. It enables you to listen to RealAudio sound and watch RealVideo video, both of which play as they download. There's no waiting around – you start hearing or seeing the clip a few seconds after you click the link.

RealAudio is often used to transmit radio shows, news bulletins and special events over the Internet. Sound quality deteriorates when the Internet is very busy, but generally it's pretty good, especially for voice broadcasts. Music doesn't transmit as well, but you can certainly tell what you're listening to. Sites that sell CDs often have RealAudio clips of sample tracks so you can check that you're buying the right disc.

There are several other add-ons that stream sound and video, but RealPlayer is the most popular.

RealVideo gives you pictures as well as sound, but doesn't work quite as well over dial-up connections. The pictures are small and fuzzy, and it can be difficult to work out what's happening. However, there's still something exciting about using the Internet to tune into a television signal from the other side of the world. Use the Sites menu to find a broadcast, or visit RealNetworks' RealGuide, at:
http://realguide.real.com/

Get RealPlayer from the RealNetworks Web site at:
http://www.real.com/

Shockwave

Macromedia's Shockwave players add some visual pizazz to the Web. Shockwave Flash is used for animations, while Shockwave Director gives you access to sophisticated multimedia presentations. It enables Internet Explorer to display files created with Director, an authoring package used to create multimedia CDs.

Flash animations are very compact, download quickly and can include interactive elements, such as buttons that react when you point or click. They're often used to add movement to the main page of a Web site.

Director movies are more complex and take longer to download. They can combine text, graphics, animation, digital video, sound and interactive elements, and most are created by professional designers who know how to get the best out of the software. You're most likely to find them on entertainment sites.

Macromedia's Shockrave site catalogues the best 'shocked' sites and is great fun to explore. Find it at:
http://www.shockrave.com/

Both the Shockwave players are included with Internet Explorer, so you'll only need to download them when Macromedia releases updates. Find out more from:
http://www.macromedia.com/

Beatnik

Beatnik is a music plug-in from Beatnik, Inc. It lets you play MIDI files – a very compact type of music file – and its own RMF (Rich Music Format) files.

MIDI files are a kind of electronic sheet music. Whereas most other types of sound file contain a recording of an actual performance, MIDI files consist of instructions for the synthesiser built in to your sound card. By telling it what notes to play, for how long, and at what volume, they enable it to make music.

The Beatnik player is a software synthesiser that can combine downloaded sound samples with standard sounds from its soundbank. The advantage of this approach is that once you've got all the sounds, Beatnik can mix them together in many ways to create lengthy songs.

Beatnik can also react to your mouse movements and clicks, enabling you to create music interactively. For example, this guitar plays a different note as the mouse pointer moves across each string.

The player is easier to use than it is to explain, and you'll enjoy finding out what it can do. Download it from:
http://www.beatnik.com/

IPIX

The IPIX viewer, produced by Interactive Pictures Corporation, enables you to 'step inside' 360-by-360-degree panoramic images. It creates the illusion that you are standing in the middle of a scene, able to spin round and look in any direction. You can also zoom in or out, and sometimes there are hotspots that take you on to other images. IPIX images are used to show you everything from the interiors of houses, hotels and museums to the cockpit of the space shuttle.

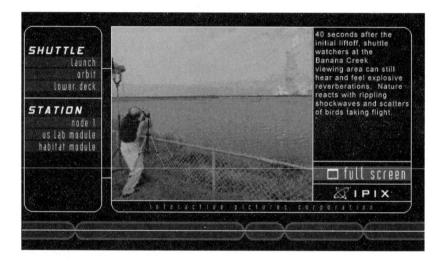

Find out more from the IPIX home page at:
`http://www.ipix.com/`

There are several other formats for panoramic images. The one you're most likely to encounter is QuickTime VR (Virtual Reality), which requires Apple's QuickTime movie player. Find out more from:
`http://www.apple.com/quicktime/qtvr/`

Viscape

Superscape's Viscape is a VRML (Virtual Reality Modelling Language) viewer that enables you to explore 3D worlds and objects. You can also view worlds created in Superscape's own SVR format.

Viscape interprets VRML files, enabling you to move around in a virtual environment and view scenes and objects from any angle. Moving around takes practice, because mice are really only designed for 2D navigation, and the 'reality' is still very obviously virtual. Nevertheless, there are lots of 3D worlds on the Web, and they're fun to explore.

This virtual reality view of the solar system comes from the *National Geographic* Web site – see page 79.

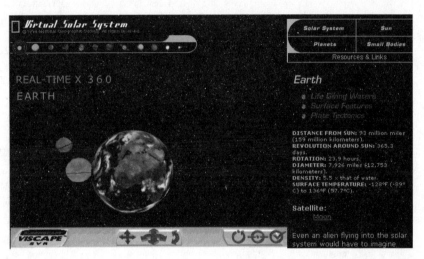

Find out more about Viscape from Superscape's site at:
`http://www.superscape.com/`

Find 3D worlds on the Virtual World Wide Web at:
`http://vwww.com/`

Acrobat

Adobe's Acrobat Reader is a page-viewing tool that enables you to browse documents saved as PDF (Portable Document Format) files. This format preserves the layout of a document as well as its content, so the copy you see on your screen looks the same as a printed copy of the original file. You can't edit the PDF version, but you can read or print it – even if you don't have the original application.

PDF files are used to distribute electronic versions of brochures and forms. They look good and print out well, so they're a popular choice when presentation is important. They also make it easy for companies to put existing documents on the Web.

Once you've installed Acrobat Reader, PDF files can be viewed from within Internet Explorer. The two programs work together, displaying both sets of tools in the same window, so you can jump from a Web page to a PDF file without switching applications.

You'll find Acrobat versions of 3Com's modem brochures on its UK Web site – see page 94.

Find out more from Adobe's Web site at:
`http://www.adobe.com/`

WebAccessories

WebAccessories are another way of extending Internet Explorer. They add new toolbar buttons, menu options or Explorer bars, enabling you to do more with your browser.

WebAccessories are usually installed like plug-ins: you download the setup program to your hard disk, then run it to install the Accessory (see pages 41 and 118).

You can find out more about WebAccessories from:
`http://www.microsoft.com/windows/ie/webaccess/`

Extra menu options

Microsoft's programmers have created a set of eight WebAccessories that add new options to the Links bar and the pop-up menu that appears when you right-click a Web page. The extra tools are:

 There's also a separate Accessory that adds a Toolbar Wallpaper option to your Tools menu. It enables you to personalise Internet Explorer's toolbars with a pattern or picture. You couldn't call it useful, but it is fun.

1   Open Frame in New Window: select any frame (see page 103) and display it in a window of its own.

2   Quick Search: lets you select your favourite engine when searching from the Address bar (see page 59).

3   Zoom In/Zoom Out: for a closer view of images.

4   Image Toggler: turn off the images so Web pages download more quickly.

5   Text Highlighter: for marking interesting passages on long Web pages.

6   Web Search: lets you select a word from a Web page, then send it to the default search engine as a keyword.

7   Links List: lists all the links on the current page.

8   Image List: a tool for Web designers. It displays all the images from the current page, with their sizes in bytes and pixels.

Extra Explorer bars

Add-on Explorer bars are displayed at the left-hand side of the Internet Explorer window, or across the bottom. Some give you access to additional search engines and other on-line tools, while others display up-to-the-minute headlines, sports results and stock quotes as you browse.

For example, AltaVista's AV Tracker displays breaking news and provides shortcuts to its shopping directory, search engine and stock quotes service.

See page 69 for more on AltaVista, and page 74 for *The New York Times* Web site.

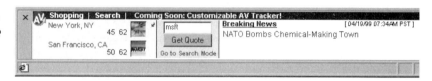

The New York Times' Explorer bar offers news headlines and stock quotes. It also has shortcuts to the main sections of the paper's Web site.

Internet Explorer 5 is the first version to support third-party Explorer bars. It remains to be seen how many bars will be produced and how useful they will be.

Once you've opened an Explorer bar, it stays open, no matter where you go on the Web, so its information and services are always accessible.

1   To turn on an extra bar that you've installed, select it from the Explorer bars section of the View menu.

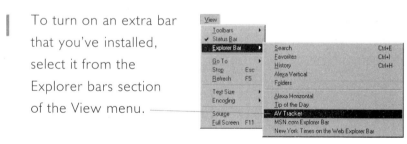

2   To turn the bar off, click the Close button (**×**) in the top left corner.

Internet Security

This chapter discusses the vexing questions of Internet security and on-line pornography. You'll learn how to protect your computer from viruses and hackers, and find out what you can do to make the Internet safe for children.

Covers

Chapter Seven

Security

When you connect your computer to the Internet, you're able to access a great wealth of information. Unfortunately, you also expose your own data to hackers and viruses.

The prospect of losing important information makes many people dubious about purchasing a modem. In reality, though, your files are more likely to be destroyed by errors and hardware failures, and you probably do a dozen potentially unsafe things every day. There are risks associated with using the Internet, and it's a good idea to be aware of them, but it isn't difficult to keep them at a manageable level. Internet Explorer's Security zones (see page 133) make it easy to select sensible security settings for several types of Web site.

If you use your computer to store information that is confidential, irreplaceable or valuable to others, consult a security expert before connecting it to the Internet. On the other hand, if losing the contents of your hard disk would merely be irritating and inconvenient, you can protect yourself against most types of attack by making regular backups of important files. In either case, following the advice given over the next few pages will reduce the chances of anything going wrong.

Viruses

If it can't make copies of itself, it isn't a virus. Rogue programs that do not replicate are called 'trojans'.

A computer virus is a small piece of program code that attaches itself to other programs. When you run the infected program, the virus copies itself to another program or causes your computer to do something untoward. Some are harmless but irritating; others may damage or destroy your files.

You can only 'catch' a computer virus by running an infected program. As well as checking all the software you download, you should be wary of programs attached to e-mails and newsgroup messages.

Software that is incomplete, badly written or simply incompatible with one of your other applications can also upset your computer. The more you download, the more important it is to make backups.

Protect yourself by investing in antivirus software and updating it regularly. It's also a good idea to establish a schedule for backing up files that contain important information or would be difficult to replace. Download files from large, well-managed file archives or directly from the company concerned, and be suspicious of anything sent to you by a stranger.

Macro viruses

Files that may contain macros, such as Microsoft Word and Excel documents, can also carry viruses. Macro viruses are a particularly sneaky development, because the files they infect don't look like programs. They've become very common in recent years and even documents from reputable sources may be infected.

Recent versions of Word and Excel can protect you against macro viruses (see the HOT TIP).

To avoid macro viruses, select Options from Word or Excel's Tools menu, then click the General tab. Make sure the 'Macro virus protection' checkbox is selected.

If you're using an older version that doesn't have this option, use a virus checker on any Word or Excel files you receive before you open them.

Authenticode

It's impossible to make the most of the Web without downloading lots of add-ons (see Chapter 6). However, it's difficult to be sure whether you're downloading a useful utility that will enhance your Web browsing or a rogue program designed to attack your system. There's also the risk that a genuine program might have been sabotaged somewhere along its journey.

To counter these fears, Microsoft has developed a system called Authenticode that helps you decide whether you can safely install an add-on. It enables publishers to add a 'digital signature' to their software, so you can be sure of its origin. These signatures are the on-line equivalent of the holograms attached to Microsoft's software boxes – they demonstrate that the application is genuine.

The digital signature takes the form of a certificate that verifies the identity of the publisher of the program. The presence of a certificate also proves that the program hasn't been tampered with along the way.

Authenticode works for programs that are installed from within Internet Explorer. If you save an installation file on to your hard disk instead of selecting Open to run it straight away, you won't see the certificate.

When you download an upgrade or add-on, you'll be shown its certificate before it is installed. If it's unsigned, you'll get a warning message instead.

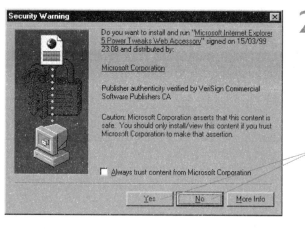

2 Click Yes to continue the installation or No if you don't have confidence in the publisher.

Virus hoaxes

There are a number of virus hoaxes that do the rounds by e-mail. The best-known example is a message that tells you not to open messages with 'Good Times' in the subject line. Doing so will delete your files and destroy your processor – or so the story goes.

This is nonsense, because you cannot catch a virus from a text-only e-mail message. However, the Good Times hoax is almost as troublesome as a real virus, because people waste a lot of time sending the message to their friends, calling their systems manager and so on.

If you receive a warning that you think might be a hoax, don't pass it on 'just in case'. You'll get your less knowledgeable friends worried over nothing, and those with more experience will think you're gullible.

How can you tell whether a virus warning is a hoax? You should be suspicious of any warning message that:

1   Contains lots of exclamation marks!!!!!

2   Tells you something dreadful will happen if you open an e-mail message with a particular title.

3   Promises total destruction of your hard disk, your processor, your entire computer, your home...

4   References a technical-sounding organisation you've never heard of and can't find on the Web.

5   Encourages you to pass it on to all your friends.

You can find out whether your message is a well-known hoax by looking it up on one of the following Web sites:

ICSA Hoax (Alert) Information, at:
`http://www.icsa.net/services/consortia/anti-virus/alerthoax.shtml`

CIAC Internet Hoaxes, at:
`http://ciac.llnl.gov/ciac/CIACHoaxes.html`

Chain letters and scams

It's an unfortunate fact of Internet life that the ease with which you can send e-mail or create Web pages encourages some people to abuse these services. You shouldn't believe everything you read on the Web, and you certainly shouldn't take every e-mail message seriously.

Chain letters

There are two sorts of chain letter. One type has a list of names and promises you enormous wealth if you send a small sum of money to the person at the top. You're then supposed to add your name to the bottom and redistribute the message. It's mathematically impossible for most of these schemes to pay off, and they're probably illegal. Many service providers will close your account if they catch you forwarding this kind of junk.

The other type promises you good luck if you forward it to all your friends, and bad luck if you don't. Some of these messages are very unpleasant, and you should delete them. You are not doing your friends any favours by sending them messages that threaten all sorts of dire consequences if they 'break the chain'.

The Craig Shergold story is an urban legend – a tale that keeps being told, regardless of its veracity. You can find many more in The AFU & Urban Legends Archive, at: `http://www.urbanlegends.com/`

There are also some well-meaning chain letters that ask you to send cards to a sick child – usually Craig Shergold, a boy with cancer – who is trying to get into *The Guinness Book of Records*. There's actually some truth to this story, which dates back to the late 1980s. However, Craig got his record, had an operation and got on with his life, so there's no need to send a card. The organisations mentioned in the letter receive quite enough unwanted mail already.

Scams

There are numerous scams circulating the Internet, some of which are quite convincing. Be suspicious of anything that sounds too good to be true, and learn to recognise the most common tricks.

Internet ScamBusters is a good source of information and advice, and issues regular newsletters. Find it at: `http://www.scambusters.org/`

Other hazards

If someone reports a serious weakness in Internet Explorer, Microsoft releases a 'patch' – a small upgrade that fixes the problem. Download the latest patches from its Security site at:
`http://www.microsoft.com/windows/ie/security/`

Internet Explorer's warnings are just that – warnings. It isn't telling you that what you want to do *will* cause a problem, just that it *might.* It's up to you to decide whether there's genuine cause for concern.

Almost all the things that make Web sites interesting can also be abused to cause you problems. Scripts, Java applets and ActiveX Controls can all potentially be used to attack your computer, although so far the risks seem more theoretical than actual. People keep discovering different ways these technologies can be used to steal passwords or monitor your browsing, but the reports are coming from researchers rather than victims.

Trying to make an accurate assessment of the risks to your computer will give you a headache. Most on-line activities are potentially dangerous, but then so are most kitchen implements. The problem is compounded by the fact that your confidence will vary from site to site. You probably trust well-known companies to produce 'safe' Web sites, but you might have a few qualms about the skills and intentions of a complete unknown.

To make things simpler, Internet Explorer provides four security settings – High, Medium, Medium-Low and Low. These settings cover all kinds of interactive content, plus file downloads and communication with insecure sites (see page 135). The High setting prevents you from downloading anything that could cause problems, keeping you safe but cutting you off from some of the more exciting aspects of the Web. Medium is less draconian: it bans some unsafe content, and warns you about the rest. Medium-Low is the same, but without the warnings. It's basically a rejigged Medium setting for people who always ignore the warning messages. Finally, the Low setting enables anyone and everyone to mess with your computer.

Rather than making you use the same setting for every site you visit, Internet Explorer divides the Internet into four 'zones': Local Intranet (your company's internal network), Trusted, Internet and Restricted. Initially all Web sites are in the Local Intranet or Internet zones (if you connect with a modem, they'll all be in the Internet zone). As you gain experience, you can add sites to the Trusted ('safe') and Restricted ('unsafe') zones. Internet Explorer will then be more lenient or more protective when you visit those sites.

It only takes a couple of minutes to decide what level of protection you require and select an appropriate security setting. You can then let Internet Explorer do the worrying and get on with browsing the Web.

1   To choose a security setting, go to Tools>Internet Options, then click the Security tab.

2   Choose the Internet zone.

If you're a security expert user, you can fine-tune your security setting by clicking Custom. This option enables you to select the types of content you want to allow and avoid.

3   Move the slider to High (at the top) to eliminate potential hazards.

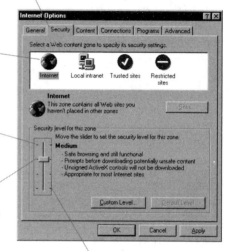

4   Medium security exposes you to some risks, but enables you to enjoy interactive Web content. You receive warnings about potential hazards. Medium-Low is the same, but without the warning messages.

5   Low security is only recommended for sites on your company network.

If you're using Internet Explorer at work, your systems manager may have added some sites to the Trusted and Restricted zones. If not, it's up to you to decide which sites fall in these categories.

1   To add a site to the Trusted or Restricted zone, click the appropriate icon, then click Sites. Enter the address and click Add. Click OK to finish.

On-line shopping

As well as protecting the data on your computer, you need to think about the information you transmit over the Internet. You probably don't care whether the keywords you submit to search engines can be intercepted (and it's unlikely a hacker would bother), but you won't want to share your credit-card number with other Internet users.

 Do not enter your credit-card number into insecure forms or include it in e-mail messages. The same rules apply to any other confidential information.

Internet shopping is generally regarded as fairly safe *as long as* you stick to reputable companies that use secure servers to collect your details. When you're connected to a secure server, all the data you send is encrypted to protect it from eavesdroppers.

There are several ways to identify a secure server:

1 Internet Explorer normally informs you that you're opening a secure connection.

2 Secure addresses begin with `https://` rather than `http://`.

3 A padlock icon (🔒) appears towards the right-hand end of the Status bar.

 **If a Web site uses frames (see page 103), it's hard to tell which sections are secure. Right-click within a frame and select Properties to check whether the connection *for that frame* is secure.**

4 Double-click the padlock to see the site's security certificate.

5 Internet Explorer will display another warning when you leave the secure server.

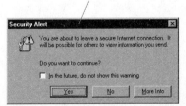

You may have to pay duty and VAT on items bought from overseas Web sites. The Customs and Excise publication *Notice 143: A Guide for International Post Users* explains the rules. Find it on the Customs and Excise Web site at `http://www.hmce.gov.uk/`

You can also protect yourself by sticking to a few simple rules when you're shopping on-line.

1   Give your money to companies you're familiar with, or whose Web sites have been recommended by people you trust.

2   Look around before you buy. Can you find the company's street address and phone number? How much will delivery cost? Will the company take your goods back if there's a problem? Good shopping sites provide plenty of information about their services.

3   If you aren't sure about a company, request a catalogue or make contact over the phone.

4   Print out details of your order (see page 46), and keep any confirmation e-mails you receive.

5   Check your credit-card statement each month and make sure you can account for all the purchases.

6   Choose a different password for each shopping site, and keep these passwords secret. Many sites keep a record of your details, which is very convenient if you make regular purchases. However, it also enables anyone who knows your password to enjoy an afternoon's shopping at your expense. See opposite for more on passwords.

Internet shopping can save you time and money and enable you to buy things you wouldn't normally get in the shops. Don't be put off by all these warnings – if you shop sensibly, it's probably safer than walking down the street with a bulging wallet in your back pocket.

Passwords

Passwords are the bane of Internet users' lives. If you aren't thinking one up for a site you've just discovered, you're probably trying to recall the one you chose last week.

Choosing passwords

There are two common ways for someone to break your password: they can guess it, or they can use a program that works through a dictionary, trying every word. Try to choose passwords that are immune to both types of attack. Don't use your name, your partner's name, your date of birth or any other easily obtainable information. Where possible, choose a mixture of numbers and letters, and make each password at least six characters long.

Remembering passwords

 Never reveal the password that you use to connect to the Net to anyone you meet on-line, even if they say they work for your service provider and need your details to prevent a problem with your account. Anyone who asks for this information is up to no good.

If you log on to the Internet from home and lead a fairly blameless life, choosing good passwords is often less important than finding some way to remember the ones you've already picked.

Internet Explorer can remember many passwords for you. It doesn't do this by default; rather, it asks if you want this feature turned on the first time you type a password into a Web site. If you click Yes, it will offer to remember each password you enter.

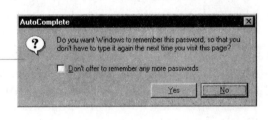

You'll probably want to use this feature for sites where your password simply gives you access. It's less of a good thing on shopping sites, especially if your computer is set up to remember your log-on password (see page 23).

> To turn this feature off, go to Tools>Internet Options. Click the Content tab, then click the AutoComplete button. Deselect the 'User names and passwords' option. You can also clear the password list.

Pornography

Talk to someone who has never used the Internet, and they will almost certainly ask you about pornography. They might not know what the Internet is or how it works, but reading the papers has given them the impression that every other Web page contains X-rated material – or worse.

 Most adult sites have no desire to provide pornographic material to children. They usually have warnings on the front page and many require credit-card details as part of the registration process.

Truthfully, there is a lot of adult material on the Internet. Most of it is perfectly legal, although not to everyone's taste; some of it is deeply unpleasant and definitely illegal in this country. The global nature of the Internet, combined with the speed at which sites come and go, makes it almost impossible to eradicate illegal images. As for the rest, the problem is not so much that it is there, but that anyone can access it – including children.

If you have a family, you are probably concerned about the sort of material your children might encounter. At the same time, there are many excellent, child-friendly Web sites. Preventing your children from accessing the Internet may protect them from inappropriate material, but it also cuts them off from all kinds of useful information.

 Internet Explorer has its own filtering system, the Content Advisor (find the controls under Tools>Internet Options>Content). However, it only works when Web designers have added ratings to their pages, and most don't. You can't rely on it to protect your children.

There's no easy way to have the 'good' bits of the Internet without also enabling a computer-savvy child to find some of the 'bad' bits. However, there are several things you can do to minimise the risks. First, install the computer in a family room, so you can keep an eye on the screen, and don't let young children browse on their own. Second, make sure your children know that they shouldn't give out personal details, such as your address or phone number.

Third, you can install filtering programs. These usually do two things: they prevent your children from accessing sites that appear on their blacklist, and they filter out pages containing forbidden words and phrases. Popular filtering programs include:

Cyber Patrol, from The Learning Company at:
`http://www.cyberpatrol.com/`

SurfWatch, from SurfWatch Software at:
`http://www.surfwatch.com/`

Working off-line

Worried about your phone bill? This chapter explains how you can save money by reloading pages you've visited previously without logging on again. You'll also learn how to make sure your favourite sites can be browsed this way.

Chapter Eight

Covers

Why work off-line?

If you connect to the Internet with a modem, you're adding to your phone bill every second you're on-line. You can reduce the damage by avoiding the expensive daytime period, signing up for discount schemes and/or switching to a telephone company that offers special rates for Internet calls. However, you'll still run up substantial bills if you use the Internet a lot.

One of the easiest ways to keep your bill down is to do as much as possible without actually logging on. For example, you don't need to be on-line while you're composing e-mail messages (see page 151). It's more economical to write all your letters off-line, then log on for a few seconds to dispatch them and download any incoming messages.

Less obviously, you can reload Web pages without connecting to the Internet. This is possible because Internet Explorer stores everything you download – Web pages, images, sound files and so on – in the Temporary Internet Files folder on your hard disk. When you click the Back button, or move on to a page that reuses some of the images from the one you've just left, Internet Explorer reloads the files from this folder instead of downloading them again. This speeds things up and makes browsing less onerous.

The files in the Temporary Internet Files folder are still accessible when you log off, and you can load them back into Internet Explorer without logging on again. You can only load pages you've already visited – if you click a link to a page you haven't seen before, Internet Explorer will have to reconnect to display it. However, if you just want to check a fact that you looked up earlier, reloading the page from your hard disk saves you the price of a call to your service provider.

The Temporary Internet Files folder

The Temporary Internet Files folder is more commonly (and more concisely) known as the cache, because it's an area for stockpiling Web pages. You'll find it in your Windows folder.

If you examine the Temporary Internet Files folder with Windows Explorer, you'll find it contains a number of strangely named subfolders. This is normal – the strange names are a security measure. You may also notice that each subfolder seems to contain the same files, giving you multiple copies of each Web page, image file and so on. *This is an illusion.* No matter which folder you click, Windows Explorer lists all the files stored anywhere within the cache, but you only have one copy of each file. Windows Explorer just likes to show you the big picture.

You can decide how much Internet Explorer should rely on your cache and how much hard-disk space it should occupy.

A 50Mb cache will only hold about 10Mb of files. PCs don't store small files efficiently, so you end up with a lot of wasted space.

1 Go to Tools>Internet Options. Click the Settings button in the Temporary Internet Files section of the General page.

2 'Automatically' is the best option for most people. If you want to be sure you're always seeing the most up-to-date material, select 'Every visit...' instead. You'll browse more slowly.

It's a good idea to clean out your cache occasionally. Go to Tools>Internet Options>General and click the Delete Files button in the Temporary Internet Files section.

3 Adjust the slider to determine how much hard-disk space is used.

4 If you want to move the folder to your D: drive, use this button. *Don't* try to move it with Windows Explorer.

Working off-line

The Work Offline option enables you to reload pages from the Temporary Internet Files folder. Normally Internet Explorer would connect to the Internet and check for updates; selecting Work Offline forces it to make do with the material in the cache.

If you are on-line, selecting Work Offline does not disconnect you – you must log off as well (see page 24).

1 Select File>Work Offline. An off-line icon () appears in the Status bar.

2 Open the Favorites bar. Pages that can be reloaded are shown in black; the rest are greyed out.

3 Select the page you want to reload.

You can also select the page you want to return to from the Favorites menu or the History bar.

If you often want to work off-line, it's a good idea to use a blank page as your Home Page (see page 57). This stops Internet Explorer from connecting to the Internet as soon as you run it.

4 If you point to a page or link that isn't available, a 'no-go' icon (🖑⊘) appears next to the cursor. Clicking produces an error message that gives you the option to log on again.

5 Deselect File>Work Offline to return to normal operation.

Making pages available

Being able to go back to the Web pages you looked at yesterday is very handy, but it doesn't help you keep up with today's news. What you really want is to be able to download all the pages you look at regularly and put them straight into the Temporary Internet Files folder, ready for off-line browsing. This is precisely what the Make Available Offline command enables you to do.

Making pages available off-line can save you money. You'll spend less time on-line, because all the minutes you normally spend reading the text and deciding where to go next are eliminated. In a typical browsing session, your modem is idle a good proportion of the time; using the off-line browsing approach, it works at full capacity for a few minutes, after which you can log off and read the downloaded pages at your leisure.

Off-line browsing is also handy if you have a portable computer. You can download your favourite pages before you leave for work, then browse through them on the train.

1 To make pages available for off-line browsing, go to Favorites > Organize Favorites.

2 Find a site you visit regularly. Select it, then select the Make Available Offline checkbox.

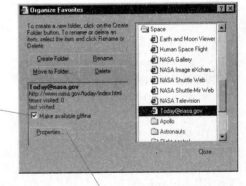

3 The front page of a news site often lists the latest headlines, then provides links to the full stories. To make Internet Explorer follow the links, click the Properties button.

...cont'd

Don't go more than one link deep unless the site has very few links on each page.

4 Click the Download tab.

5 Set 'Download pages...' to one link deep.

6 Decide whether you want to follow links to pages on other servers.

7 If you're short of disk space, you may want to set a limit for this site.

If in doubt, follow external links and don't set a limit for the site. You can come back and change these options later if there's a problem.

8 Click the Advanced button for more options.

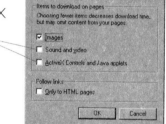

9 You probably don't want to download sounds, videos, ActiveX Controls and Java applets, because they can be very large.

You can also right-click on a site's entry in the Favorites menu or bar and select **Make Available Offline.** You'll be asked a series of questions that cover the same ground as the boxes shown here.

10 Click OK twice to go back to the Organize Favorites dialogue box.

11 Repeat steps 2–10 for other sites you want to download.

Selecting the 'Make available offline' checkbox marks a site for download. The files aren't actually fetched until you tell Internet Explorer to synchronise the pages in your cache with the ones on the Internet (it may do this spontaneously when you first select a site).

Synchronising

When you synchronise your computer, Internet Explorer checks whether the pages you've selected have been updated and downloads any new material.

1 Go to the Tools menu and select Synchronize.

To change any of the details you entered when you marked a page, click the name of the site, then click Properties.

2 Click the checkboxes of the sites you want to download.

3 Click Synchronize.

4 Internet Explorer checks for updates and downloads any pages that have changed.

If your computer is on a network that's permanently connected to the Internet, you can schedule sychronisations for the middle of the night. Click the Setup button to do this.

5 When Internet Explorer has finished, log off. Select Work Offline and use the Favorites menu, the Favorites bar or the History bar to browse your pages (see page 142).

Problems?

Off-line browsing doesn't always work as advertised, and sometimes you end up wasting more connection time than you save.

If you find that very few of the pages listed in the History bar can be accessed off-line, try increasing the size of the cache (see page 141). If that doesn't help, pay a visit to EnigmaticSoftware (`http://www.mindspring.com/~dpoch/enigmatic/`) and download a copy of its CacheSentry utility. Internet Explorer isn't very good at deciding which files to delete when the cache gets full, and sometimes it throws away new files rather than old ones. CacheSentry fixes this problem and can make a marked difference to the number of recently visited pages you can access off-line.

You'll still find that some pages can't be accessed off-line. Sometimes it's because you didn't allow the page to download completely before you clicked a link and moved on. Web designers can also specify that a page shouldn't be cached. Usually they do this because the page changes frequently and they want to make sure people always see the latest version. Finally, some pages don't cache for technical reasons to do with the way they're constructed.

The facility to download linked pages can be a mixed blessing. Most Web sites aren't designed with this kind of browsing in mind, and you can end up downloading a lot of material you wouldn't have bothered with if you had browsed the site on-line.

Sometimes the problem sorts itself out after a couple of synchronisations – you download superfluous pages such as copyright notices the first time, then Internet Explorer just updates the pages that change. Often, however, there'll be new material that interests you, and new material that doesn't, but no way to have one without the other. If you end up ignoring most of the material you've downloaded, you're better off synchronising individual pages or browsing the site on-line.

Electronic mail

This chapter introduces Outlook Express, the e-mail program supplied with Internet Explorer. It shows you how to send and receive messages, add special formatting and attach files. It also explains how to keep track of addresses, sort and file your mail and set up e-mail accounts for all the family.

Chapter Nine

Covers

E-mail explained

E-mail is short for electronic mail, the Internet equivalent of letters and faxes. It's better than either, though, not only because it's quick and cheap, but also because you can attach files to an e-mail message. This means you can send text documents, pictures, sound samples and program files as well as simple messages.

You can send e-mail to anyone on the Internet; you just need to know their address, which will look something like:

johndoe@someplace.co.uk

The part before the @ is the recipient's user name.

The part after the @ is the address of the recipient's service provider.

When you send an e-mail message, it is delivered to the recipient's service provider very quickly – usually within a few minutes. It is stored in the recipient's mail box until he or she next logs on and checks for new e-mail.

E-mail is very efficient if you're dealing with someone who checks their mail box regularly, but not so good for getting messages to people who only log on once a week. It's handy for contacting people who are perpetually on the phone or out of the office, and makes it easier to deal with people in different time zones. Instead of calling at an awkward hour, you can have a message waiting for them when they arrive at work.

You can also have daily news bulletins and other useful information delivered to your mail box. E-mail might not get as much media coverage as the Web, but it's at least as useful and a lot less time-consuming.

Introducing Outlook Express

Outlook Express is a program for accessing e-mail and Usenet newsgroups (see Chapter 10). It has a few things in common with the Outlook application supplied with Microsoft Office, but don't get the two mixed up. Beneath the surface they are very different, and things that work in one won't necessarily work in the other. Outlook Express is optimised for sending mail over the Internet and should have been included with your copy of Internet Explorer.

You should also be able to run Outlook Express from Internet Explorer – click the Mail button and select Read Mail. If this doesn't work, go to Tools>Internet Options. Click the Programs tab and make sure 'E-mail:' is set to 'Outlook Express'.

1   To run Outlook Express, double-click its icon.

2   If you didn't fill in your e-mail details when you installed Internet Explorer, you'll be prompted to set up your account (see pages 21–22).

Outlook Express

3   Outlook Express will probably connect to the Internet and check for new messages. Once it has finished, log off and click the Inbox icon.

Outlook bar

Folder list – folders for all your messages

Folder bar – shows name of current folder

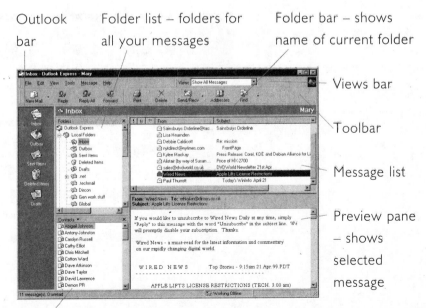

Views bar

Toolbar

Message list

Preview pane – shows selected message

Contacts list – names from the Address book

Your Outlook Express window won't look exactly the same as the one on the previous page – you won't have as many folders or messages, and you may not see all the items. There are lots of different ways to organise this window.

1   Select Layout from the View menu.

2   Select the items you want to display.

3   Click Customize Toolbar to add or remove toolbar buttons or change the button size.

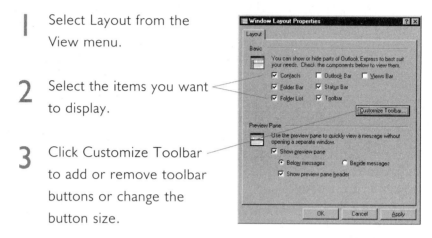

4   You can also change the relative sizes of most of the items by dragging the grey dividing bars.

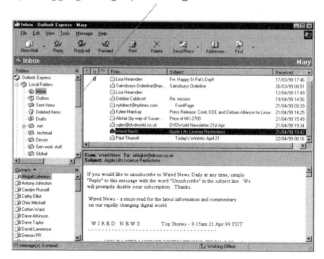

Sending e-mail

You have to be connected to the Internet to send a message, but you don't have to be on-line while you compose it. It's best to write your messages before you log on, then send them all in a batch. You can collect any new messages at the same time (see page 155).

 Some Web pages have special links that produce a New Message window with the address already filled in.

 To send the same message to several people, enter all their addresses, separated by semi-colons.

 If you have one of the Microsoft Office applications, you can spellcheck your message. Click the Spelling button, select Tools>Check Spelling or press F7.

1 To write a message, click the New Mail button, select Message>New Message or press Ctrl+N.

2 A New Message window appears.

3 Enter the e-mail address of the recipient.

4 Fill in the subject line.

5 Compose your message.

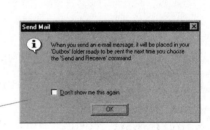

6 Click the Send button, select File>Send Message or press Alt+S. This doesn't actually send the message, it just transfers it to the Outbox.

7 When you're ready to send all your messages, click Send and Receive or press Ctrl+M. Outlook Express connects to the Internet and sends everything in your Outbox.

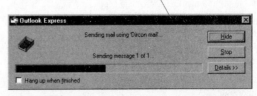

Formatted e-mail

Outlook Express enables you to use HTML commands to produce e-mail messages that look as good as Web pages.

To specify which setting should be used by default, go to Tools>Options and click the Send tab. Set the mail format to 'HTML' or 'Plain Text'.

Use the New Message window's Format menu to switch between Rich Text (HTML) and Plain Text. A formatting bar appears when Rich Text is selected.

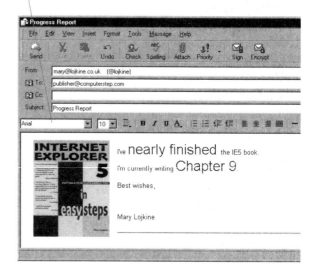

Stick to fonts that the other person will have: Arial, Comic Sans, Impact, Times New Roman and Verdana.

2 Use the drop-down lists and buttons to format your text. Use the Format menu to set the background colour, and the Insert menu for lines or pictures.

Formatted mail is fun, and handy when you're trying to catch someone's eye. However, it's only a good idea if you're sure the other person uses a program that can handle HTML mail. Formatted messages look awful in older e-mail programs, and a lot of people find them irritating. If in doubt, stick to Plain Text.

Stationery

Outlook Express comes with predesigned 'Stationery' that can add a touch of class to your correspondence or help you celebrate special occasions. As with formatted mail, though, Stationery is only a good idea if you're sure the recipient's e-mail program will display it properly.

To specify a default Stationery design, go to Tools>Options. Click the Compose tab, select 'Mail:' and pick a design.

1 To compose a new message using Stationery, click the arrow next to the New Mail button and select a design.

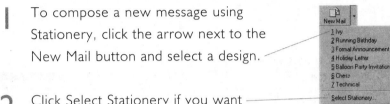

2 Click Select Stationery if you want more choices.

To design your own Stationery, go to the Compose section of the Tools>Options dialogue box. Click Create New to run the Stationery Wizard. There's also a Download More button that takes you to Microsoft's Web site, where you'll find some extra designs.

3 Complete and send your message as usual.

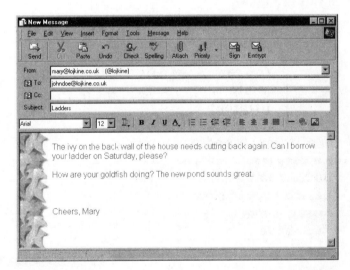

4 If you forget to select a Stationery design when you create your message, switch to Rich Text format (see opposite), then select Format>Apply Stationery.

Signatures

A signature is a short piece of text that is appended to the end of every message you send. If you're sending messages from work, it might include your contact details; otherwise you could use a personal comment or favourite quote. Keep it short, though – long ones soon become tiresome.

1 To set up a signature, go to Tools > Options and click the Signatures tab.

If you only want to sign some messages, don't select 'Add...' You'll be able to add your signature manually using Insert>Signature.

2 Select 'Add signatures to all outgoing...'

3 Click New, then click Rename to give the signature a sensible name.

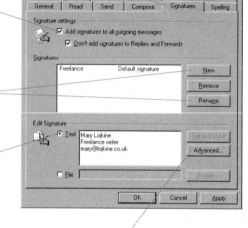

You can create different signatures for different moods or messages. Once you have more than one, it's best to sign messages manually – see above.

4 Select 'Text' and enter the text you want to use.

5 Click Advanced if you have several accounts (see page 167) and only want to use this signature with some of them.

6 The text is added to the end of every message you create.

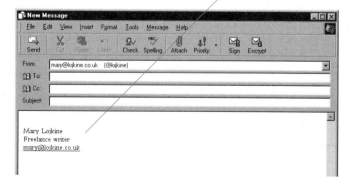

Receiving e-mail

Unlike 'real' mail, e-mail messages aren't automatically delivered to your door – or in this case, computer. When someone sends you an e-mail, it's delivered to your service provider's mail server, which puts it into your personal mail box. You must then log on and collect it.

1   To check your mail box, click Send and Receive. Outlook Express connects to the Internet (if necessary), sends any messages that are waiting in your Outbox and fetches any new mail. The new messages are placed in your Inbox. You can log off and read them in your own time.

See page 183 to find out how to sort your incoming messages.

2   Select the Inbox folder to see a list of the messages you have received.

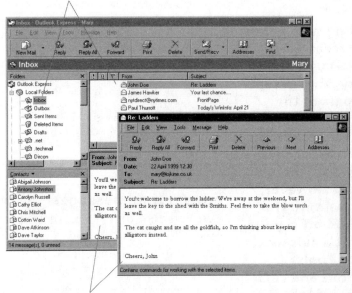

To print a message, press Print, select File>Print or press Ctrl+P.

3   Click once on a message to select it and display the text in the Preview pane at the bottom of the window, or twice to display it in a separate window.

Replying and forwarding

It's easy to reply to an e-mail message, because Internet Explorer automatically adds the correct address.

1 To reply to a message, select it, then click the Reply button. Alternatively, select Message> Reply to Sender or press Ctrl+R. Internet Explorer opens a New Message window.

2 The To: and Subject: lines are already filled in.

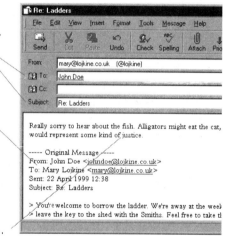

3 The text from the previous message is quoted at the bottom.

Quoting is useful when you're dealing with people who receive a lot of mail. If you delete everything except the part of the message to which you're responding, it's easy for them to see what you're on about. However, you can turn this feature off if you find it a nuisance. Go to Tools> Options and click the Send tab. Deselect 'Include message in reply'.

4 Type your reply at the top, then delete any superfluous material from the bottom section.

5 Send the message as usual (see page 151).

Forwarding messages

You can also divert an e-mail message to a friend who might find it interesting, or to someone who is better able to respond to the original sender.

1 To forward a message, select it and click the Forward button. Alternatively, select Message>Forward or press Ctrl+F. Enter the new address in the To: line.

2 Add any comments you wish to make above the quoted text, then send the message.

Attachments

You can e-mail pictures, document files and programs to your friends and colleagues. If you have a digital camera or microphone, you can bring your messages to life with snapshots or recordings. More prosaically, being able to exchange files by e-mail is very handy if you're working from home.

1 Compose your message (see page 151), then click the Attach File button. Alternatively, select File Attachment from the New Message window's Insert menu.

You can attach any kind of file, but don't send your friends large files without warning them first. You should also make sure they have the right software for viewing your files.

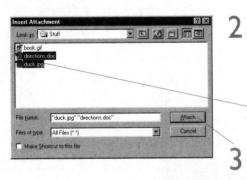

2 Find the file(s) you want to send – you can select several at once by holding down Shift or Ctrl as you click.

3 Click Attach.

4 The files are added to the message, which can be sent as usual.

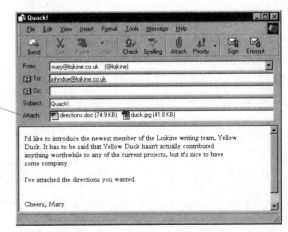

Receiving attachments

When you receive a message with attached files, you have two main choices: open the files, or save them on to your hard disk.

If you receive a file from someone you don't know (or don't trust), save it on to your hard disk and check for viruses before you open it. This goes double for Word documents, which can carry macro viruses (see page 129).

1 If you see paperclip icons in the message list and preview pane, the associated message has one or more files attached. In some cases – for example, when a .gif or .jpg image has been attached – the file is displayed at the end of the text.

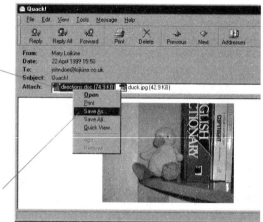

2 When you open the message, the attached files are listed at the top. Right-click a file to open or save it.

3 You can also deal with attached files by clicking the gold paperclip at the top of the Preview Pane. Click a file to open it, or click Save Attachments to save the files on to your hard disk.

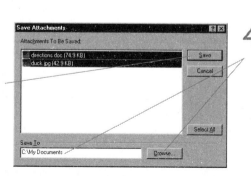

5 Select the files you want to save and click Save.

4 Click Browse and choose a folder.

Send and Receive options

Outlook Express' Options dialogue gives you control over when and how messages are sent and received.

Most of Outlook Express' options are fairly easy to understand. For more information, click the Help button (?) in the top-right corner, then click an option. If you're still stuck, the OE User Tips Home Page at http://www.okinfoweb.com/moe/ **is a great source of advice.**

1 Select Tools>Options. Click the General tab.

2 Select '...at startup' if you want Outlook Express to connect and check for new messages as soon as you run it.

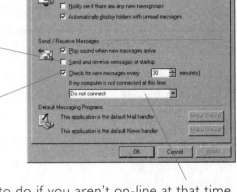

3 Select '...every xx minutes' if you want Outlook Express to check again at regular intervals. Tell it what to do if you aren't on-line at that time.

4 Click the Send tab.

5 Select '...immediately' to make Outlook Express connect and dispatch each message as soon as you click the Send button (not usually a good idea).

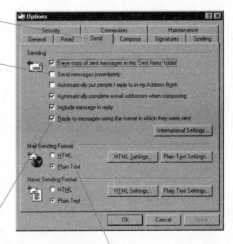

6 It's courteous to reply to messages in the sender's preferred format.

7 See page 152 for more on formatted mail.

Address Book

The Address Book enables you to store all the e-mail addresses you use regularly. You can then add them to messages more easily.

1 To open the Address Book, click the Addresses button, select Tools>Address Book or press Ctrl+Shift+B.

It's even easier to add the address of someone who has sent you an e-mail message. Select the message, then go to Tools> Add Sender to Address Book.

2 To add an address, click the New button and select New Contact. You can also select File>New Contact or press Ctrl+N.

3 Fill in the person's name.

4 Enter a nickname.

5 Enter the e-mail address and click Add. Repeat if they have several.

6 Click the Home, Business, Personal and Other tabs to add any other information you wish to record.

7 Click OK to finish.

8 You can now enter the person's name or nickname in the To: line of your messages. Outlook Express will look up the address when you send the message. Alternatively, double-click the person's entry in the Contacts list to create a preaddressed message form.

Finding Addresses

If you don't know someone's e-mail address, the easiest way to find it out is by asking them. If that isn't practical, you may be able to track them down using one of the on-line directories. These are a lot like phone books (they are sometimes called 'White Pages'), except they contain e-mail addresses rather than phone numbers.

1   Go to Edit > Find > People.

2   Choose an address service.

3   Enter the person's name and click Find Now.

4   Outlook Express connects to the Internet, searches the database you selected and displays the bottom half of the dialogue box. With luck you'll see a list of names and be able to guess which address belongs to the person you are looking for.

5   If you don't succeed, try one of the other services.

6   You might also like to visit the Web pages of the various services (just click the Web Site button) and register your details so your friends can look you up.

Managing your e-mail

Initially you have five e-mail folders: Inbox, Outbox, Sent Items, Deleted Items and Drafts.

1   New e-mail is deposited in the Inbox (see page 155).

2   Outgoing e-mail waits in the Outbox (see page 151).

3   Once a message has been dispatched, it is moved to the Sent Items folder so you have a copy.

The Deleted Items folder is like the Windows Recycle bin – it stores items you think you won't need again until you're ready to get rid of them for good. To empty the folder, select Edit> Empty 'Deleted Items' Folder.

4   If you select a message and click Delete, select Edit> Delete, press Delete or press Ctrl+D, it ends up in the Deleted Items folder. You can rescue it if necessary.

5   If you close a message without sending it, Outlook Express asks if you want to save it. If you click Yes, it is moved to the Drafts folder so you can work on it again later.

Sorting your e-mail

As well as placing your e-mail in these folders, Outlook Express enables you to sort the messages in each one.

To change the categories, right-click on any tab and select Columns...

To sort your messages, click one of the grey category tabs at the top of the list. Click again to reverse the sort.

Sorted by sender

Sorted by date received

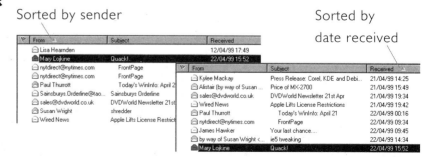

Creating your own folders

Some messages can be thrown away as soon as you've read them, but there'll be others you want to keep. You can create additional e-mail folders and file them away tidily.

1 To create a new e-mail folder, go to File>Folder>New.

2 Enter a name.

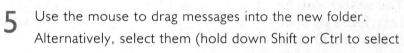

3 To create a top-level folder, select Local Folders. If you want it to be a subfolder, select one of your existing folders.

4 Click OK to add the folder to the folder list.

5 Use the mouse to drag messages into the new folder. Alternatively, select them (hold down Shift or Ctrl to select several at once), then go to Edit> Move to Folder. Select the folder and click OK.

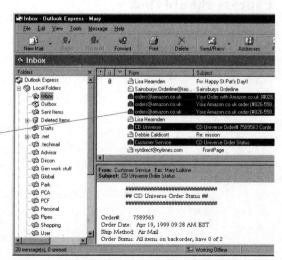

Finding messages

No matter how careful you are when you file your e-mail, there will come a day when you can't find the message where so-and-so said such-and-such. Fortunately Outlook Express has a comprehensive Find function that should be able to locate the missing message – assuming it hasn't been permanently deleted.

1 To search for a message, go to Edit>Find>Message. Alternatively, press Ctrl+Shift+F.

If you're reasonably certain that the message is in a particular folder, select it (rather than Local Folders) when you click the Browse button. The search will be restricted to that folder and Outlook Express should find the message more quickly.

2 Click the Browse button and select Local Folders to search everywhere. Make sure 'Include subfolders' is selected.

3 Enter all the details you're sure about. Use the Message: line for words that appeared in the text of the message.

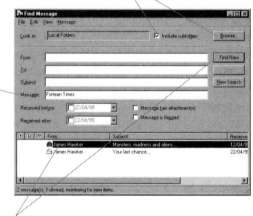

4 Click Find Now. Outlook Express searches for matching messages and lists them at the bottom of the box. Double-click a message to open it.

5 If you get a very long list of messages, enter some more information and click Find Now again. Conversely, if you don't get any matches, try entering less information. A single, well-chosen word may be all you need.

6 Click New Search if you want to clear the dialogue box and start all over again.

Message Rules

Message Rules enable you to sort your incoming messages by sender, subject or content and delete, file or reply to them automatically. They're useful for separating business and personal mail, or for blocking messages from people who keep sending you junk.

1 To create a Message Rule, go to Tools>Message Rules> Mail. Click the New button.

You can select several conditions and actions at once to create very complex Rules. The dialogue boxes that enable you to specify the details of each condition usually have Options buttons that give you even more choices. For example, you can reverse the Rule so the action is applied when the message doesn't meet your criterion.

2 Select a condition that the message must meet.

3 Select the action to be taken.

4 Click the blue, underlined text to fill in details of the condition.

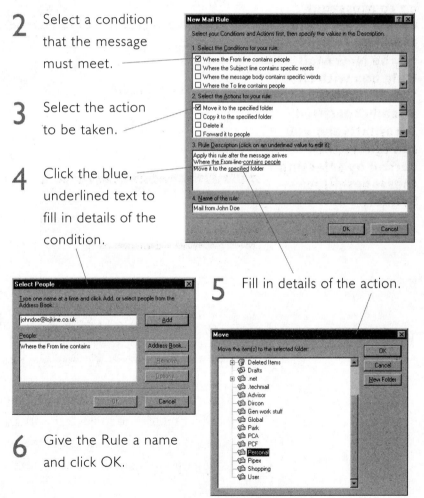

5 Fill in details of the action.

6 Give the Rule a name and click OK.

There are two easy ways to create Rules based on the sender of the message. Select a message from the correct person, then go to Message> Create Rule From Message to bring up the New Mail Rule box with the 'From' details already specified. Alternatively, you can ignore this person by selecting Messages>Block Sender.

7 All your Rules are listed in the Message Rules dialogue box.

8 Use the checkboxes to enable or disable any of your Rules.

9 Rules are applied in order. Click Move Up or Move Down to reshuffle them.

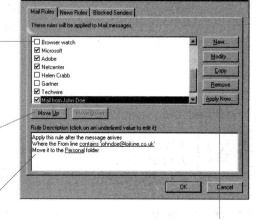

10 Click a Rule to see its details.

11 Click Apply Now to test your Rules.

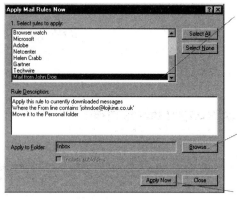

12 Select the Rule(s) you want to test.

13 Click Browse to select a folder – your Inbox is usually the best choice.

14 Click Apply Now.

15 Close all the dialogue boxes and check whether your Rule has had the desired effect. If not, go back to the Message Rules dialogue box and select the Rule. Click Modify to change the condition and/or action.

16 The active Rules (see Step 8) are applied to all your incoming mail.

Multiple accounts

This section shows you how to set up Outlook Express to handle multiple accounts belonging to the same person. Page 169 explains how to manage accounts belonging to different people.

It's quite common to have more than one e-mail account. Conventional service providers often give you several e-mail addresses, and the rise of free services has encouraged many people to sign up for several Internet accounts. There's no point getting carried away, but it is useful to have separate addresses for business and personal mail.

1   To add a new account, select Tools>Accounts. Click Add and select Mail.

2   The Internet Connection Wizard asks you questions about your account (see page 22).

3   You'll end up back at the Internet Accounts dialogue box, with your new account added to the list.

Messages are sent from your default account unless you specify otherwise.

4   Select your main account and click Set as Default.

5   To change any of the details you entered in Step 2, select the account and click Properties.

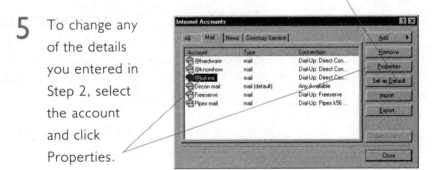

The 'Include this account...' option determines whether this account is checked when you click Send and Receive. If you only want to check it occasionally, deselect this checkbox.

6   The General section has your personal details. The name you enter here is the one people will see when you send them a message.

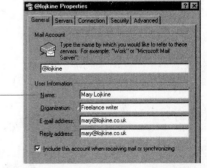

Outlook Express normally uses the default connection specified for Internet Explorer (see page 25), and that'll be fine if you only use one service provider. If you have e-mail accounts with several different service providers, you may find you have to specify the correct connection for each one.

7 The Connection section tells Outlook Express how to log on to the Internet when you click Send and Receive.

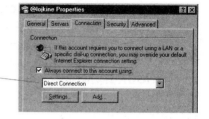

Using your accounts

You can send and receive mail from your default account in the usual way. Using secondary accounts is slightly more complicated.

1 If the 'Include this account...' option is selected (see previous page), the secondary account is checked when you click Send and Receive. If not, you need to check it manually. Go to the Tools menu and select Send and

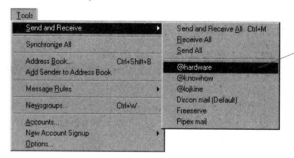

Receive, then the name of the account.

2 To send a message from a particular account, select it from the drop-down list at the top of the New Message form.

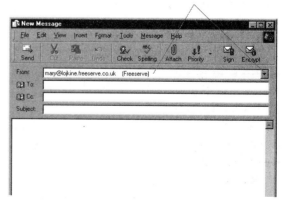

Identities

You can follow the instructions from the previous two pages to set up accounts for all the family, but you'll find that everyone's mail ends up in a heap in the Inbox. A better solution is to create several Identities. Each person can then have their own accounts, mail folders, Address Book and Message Rules. They can even change the layout of the Outlook Express window without affecting anyone else's interface. It's almost as if each person has their own copy of Outlook Express, except you only need to install the program once.

1. Go to File>Identities>Add New Identity.

2. Type your name (or the name of the person who'll use this identity).

3. If you want to keep your mail private, select the 'Ask me for a password...' checkbox. Enter a password.

Use File> Import to transfer messages and Address Books from one Identity to another. You'll find your files in C:\Windows\ Application Data\ Microsoft.

4. Click OK once or twice, as required.

5. Click Yes to switch to the new Identity.

6. The Internet Connection Wizard appears so you can create an e-mail account for the new Identity (see page 22).

...cont'd

Managing identities

Identities are really very straightforward. Once you've told Outlook Express who you are, it finds all your mail and sets things up the way you like them.

If the Folder bar is turned on (see pages 149–150 for how to activate this if necessary), it displays the name of the current Identity.

1 To choose the correct Identity, go to File>Switch Identities.

2 Select a name, enter your password (if required) and click OK.

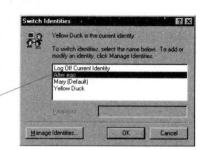

3 To determine what happens when you run Outlook Express, go to File>Identities>Manage Identities.

4 Select the start-up Identity, or select Ask Me to be prompted to choose an Identity at start-up.

When you remove an Identity, all the mail sent to that person is deleted.

5 You can also use the Manage Identities dialogue box to remove unwanted Identities.

Hotmail

Hotmail is a free e-mail system owned by Microsoft. It's designed to be used from a Web browser – the idea is that you can access your e-mail from any computer that's connected to the Internet, without having to set up an e-mail program. However, you can also download Hotmail messages into Outlook Express so you can read and respond to them off-line.

Although you can set up a new Hotmail account from within Outlook Express, it's better to go to Hotmail's Web site (`http://www.hotmail.com/`). You can then find out all about the service before you choose your user name and password. Once that's done, you can configure Outlook Express to access your new account.

 You can also tell Internet Explorer to use your Hotmail account when you click e-mail links on Web pages. Go to Tools>Internet Options>Programs and set 'E-mail:' to 'Hotmail'.

1 Follow the instructions on page 167 to start the Internet Connection Wizard. Enter your name and Hotmail address.

2 When you're asked what type of server you use, select HTTP. Select Hotmail from the drop-down list that appears.

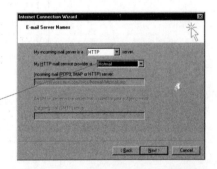

3 When you finish, you'll be asked if you want to connect and download folders from the server. Click Yes.

4 You can use your Hotmail account like any other e-mail account. However, it gets its own set of mail folders.

Making the most of e-mail

E-mail isn't just a way to bypass the postbox and fax machine. It also enables you to keep informed, join discussion groups, play games and have some fun with your friends.

The easiest way to fill your Inbox is by subscribing to a few mailing lists. There are two sorts: announcement lists that deliver regular newsletter-style messages, and discussion lists that are more like e-mail conversations. Everyone on the list submits their news, thoughts, recipes or whatever to the mail server, which copies them to all the members. They're a good way to get in touch with Internet users who share your interests.

Many of the bigger Web sites have announcement lists that tell you what has been added each week. You can usually sign up somewhere on the site – in fact, you'll often find that registering (see page 100) puts you on the list. Discussion lists may also have associated Web pages, but you usually sign up by e-mail. The best place to start is the Liszt Web site, which provides details of over 90,000 mailing lists. Find it at:
`http://www.liszt.com/`

Play-by-e-mail games are also popular. You can play almost anything, including board, strategy and role-playing games, or join a fantasy sports league. Some games work entirely by e-mail – you just submit your move and wait for a response – while others take moves by e-mail, then display the results on a Web site.

Finally, there are lots of Web sites that use e-mail to deliver useful or amusing services. You can send electronic postcards to your friends, use automatic letter writers to generate romantic or sarcastic messages, or order a (picture of) a pizza over the Web. On a more practical note, you can also sign up for reminder services that send you messages on (or just before) important dates such as birthdays and anniversaries. Go to Yahoo! (see page 68) and search for 'e-mail' or 'cards' to find out what's available.

Newsgroups explained

Chapter Ten

Usenet newsgroups

Usenet newsgroups enable you to communicate with Internet users who share your interests. This chapter shows you how to read and post messages, then explains newsgroup etiquette and customs.

Covers

Newsgroups explained

The Usenet newsgroups are the Internet equivalent of your local pub or social club. They're nowhere near as pretty as the Web, but they're more interactive. If you're looking for gossip, trivia, advice, arguments and – very occasionally – news, Usenet is the place to find it.

Newsgroup 'messages' are also referred to as 'posts' and 'articles'. The three terms are interchangeable.

You can think of a newsgroup as a public mail box for messages on a particular topic. Anyone can post a comment, and anyone else can read it and upload a reply.

Unlike Web pages, newsgroups aren't stored in any particular place. All the messages are copied from one news server to the next, enabling you to access them locally. Rather than connecting to lots of sites from all over the globe, you download the latest messages from your service provider's news server.

There are over 40,000 newsgroups, although some service providers only carry the more popular ones. Some have a close-knit community of regular posters; others are larger and more anonymous. Either way, though, there's certain to be someone who wants to share your experiences, answer your questions, ask for advice or just pass the time of day.

Understanding newsgroup names

Newsgroup addresses look like:

`rec.arts.movies.reviews`

or sometimes:

`news:rec.arts.movies.reviews`

Newsgroups are organised hierarchically: each section of the address (moving from left to right) reduces the scope of the group. In this case `rec` stands for recreation, `arts` and `movies` are self-evident and the group only carries `reviews`. There are 14 other `movies` groups, about 130 other `arts` groups, and over 800 `rec` groups in total.

`rec` is only one of dozens of top-level categories. However, you can find almost everything you're likely to want in `alt`, `comp`, `news`, `rec`, `sci`, `soc` and `uk`.

alt – alternative

Almost anyone can create an `alt` newsgroup, so the `alt` hierarchy is one of the liveliest sections of Usenet. Some of the groups are pretty wild, but most are just odd – if you're interested in alien conspiracies, urban legends or breakfast cereal, `alt` has much to offer. It's also a nursery for new groups, some of which eventually graduate to the more respectable hierarchies.

comp – computing

The `comp` groups deal with everything from hardware and software to artificial intelligence and home automation.

The name 'Usenet' is derived from 'User Network'. Usenet is a network of computers (news servers) that exchange news messages.

news – Usenet

The `news` groups are for discussion about Usenet. They aren't terribly exciting, but `news.announce.newusers` has lots of information for beginners.

rec – recreation

The `rec` groups cover hobbies, sports, arts and music, and are the best place to start. They tend to be friendlier than the `alt` groups and it's easy to find your way around.

sci – science

The `sci` groups cover mathematics, physics, engineering, chemistry, biological science, medicine, psychology and philosophy – everything except computing, basically.

soc – social

The `soc` groups deal with social issues. The biggest subsection, `soc.culture`, has over 100 groups dedicated to various countries and cultures. Genealogy, history and religion are well represented, and there are a number of support groups.

uk – United Kingdom

The `uk` groups are a microcosm of Usenet as a whole. The most popular groups are `uk.politics` and `uk.misc`, but you'll also find job ads, an *Archers* group and a selection of `rec` and `religion` groups.

Getting started

There are many similarities between sending e-mail and posting messages to newsgroups. You use Outlook Express for both, and many operations are identical. However, you will notice some changes in the menus when you switch from sending and receiving e-mail to reading news.

The first thing you need to do is find out the address of your service provider's news server and set up Outlook Express to connect to it.

1 Run Outlook Express and select Tools>Accounts. Click Add and select News.

2 Enter your name and e-mail address (Outlook Express should copy these from your default e-mail account, so you'll probably just have to click Next to okay its choices).

3 Fill in the address of your service provider's news server. You don't normally have to log on to news servers.

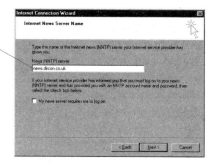

4 When you get back to the Internet Accounts dialogue box, click the News tab. You should see an entry for your news server. You may want to select Properties and give it a sensible name.

5 When you close the dialogue box, Outlook Express asks if you want to download newsgroups. Click Yes.

6 Outlook Express downloads the names of the newsgroups carried by your service provider. This takes a few minutes, but you only have to do it once.

Subscribing to a newsgroup isn't like subscribing to a magazine or joining a club. You don't have to pay, and you won't be added to a membership list. Subscribing just tells Outlook Express you're interested in a newsgroup – it's like making a Favorite for a Web site.

7 The newsgroup list appears. You now need to select some newsgroups and 'subscribe' to them.

8 Scroll down the list until you find a group that looks interesting, then select it and click the Subscribe button.

9 To find groups covering a particular subject, type a word that might appear in the name into the 'Display...' box.

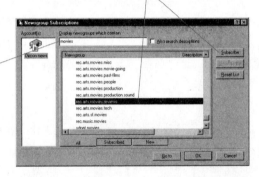

10 Click the Subscribed tab to see a list of the groups you have selected.

11 If you want to add some more groups later on, select your news server from the Folders list. Click the Newsgroups button or select Tools>Newsgroups. You won't have to download the list again – Outlook Express stores it on your hard disk.

Reading news

Reading newsgroup messages is slightly different from reading e-mail. Instead of downloading all the messages, which might take some time, Outlook Express only fetches the headers (the subject line, name of sender and so on). You can then download the ones that sound interesting.

1 Select your news server from the Folder list to display your subscribed newsgroups.

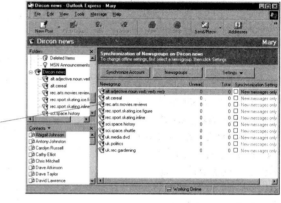

2 Double-click one of the groups to download the titles of the current messages.

Some groups are very busy and receive hundreds of new messages each day. To tell Outlook Express how many headers to fetch, select Tools> Options and click the Read tab. Enter a number in the 'Get xx headers at a time' box.

3 Click a title to download and display the body of the message.

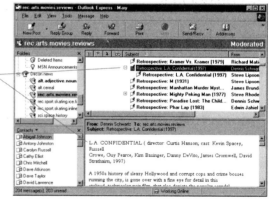

4 On-going conversations are 'threaded' – the responses are displayed immediately below the original message. Click the plus (⊞) and minus (⊟) icons to expand and contract the threads.

Posting messages

See page 184 before you start posting messages – there are lots of things that are considered rude on Usenet.

Posting messages is similar to sending e-mail (see page 151), but you address the message to the newsgroup.

1. To create a new message, first make sure you are viewing the correct newsgroup. Click New Post, select Message>New Message or press Ctrl+N.

If your response won't be of interest to anyone other than the original poster, e-mail it directly to them. Click Reply to Author, select Message>Reply to Sender or press Ctrl+R to create a preaddressed form.

2. To respond to a message, select it. Click Reply to Group, select Message>Reply to Group or press Ctrl+G.

3. Either way, Outlook Express brings up a preaddressed New Message window (if you're responding to an existing message, the original text is quoted – see page 156). Fill in the Subject line and compose your message.

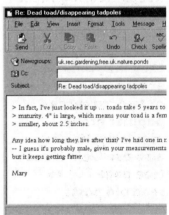

Want to practice? Post a message to the `alt.test` newsgroup.

4. Click Send, select File>Send Later or press Alt+S. This transfers the message to your Outbox.

5. Your message is uploaded to the news server when you click Send and Receive.

Working off-line

Minimise the amount of time you spend on-line by marking the messages you want to read and downloading them all at once. You can then disconnect from the Internet and read the messages off-line.

1   Select your news server from the Folder list.

News messages don't stay on the server forever; your service provider keeps clearing them out to make way for new ones. If a group is very busy, they may only be accessible for a day or two, so check popular groups regularly. You can also use Deja News (see page 70) to read old posts.

2   Select all your newsgroups, then click the Settings button and select Headers Only.

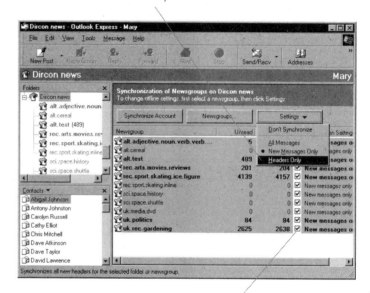

3   Deselect the checkboxes of any groups you don't want to bother with today.

4   Click Synchronize Account. Outlook Express connects to the Internet and downloads the headers of any new messages sent to any of the selected groups.

5   Log off and select Work Offline from the File menu.

6   Double-click on one of your newsgroups. Scroll down the list of messages and select one that sounds interesting.

...cont'd

If you read more than half the messages posted to a group, you're better off selecting New Messages Only (rather than Headers) in Step 2 and fetching everything. Use the Headers option at least once before you do this, though. If you don't, all the messages will be new and you might have to download thousands of them.

You can mark messages more quickly by clicking in the column where the arrows appear.

7 Mark the message for downloading. To do this, go to Tools>Mark for Offline>Download Message Later. You can also mark an entire conversation (thread), or all the messages in the group.

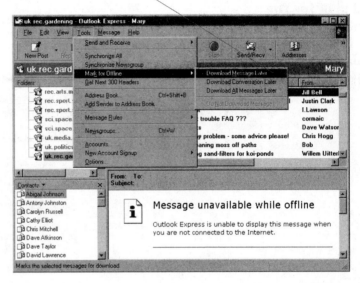
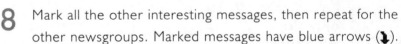
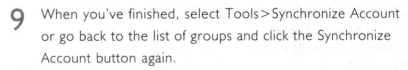

8 Mark all the other interesting messages, then repeat for the other newsgroups. Marked messages have blue arrows (↓).

9 When you've finished, select Tools>Synchronize Account or go back to the list of groups and click the Synchronize Account button again.

10 Outlook Express downloads the marked messages.

11 Log off and select Work Offline again. Select a newsgroup, then select one of the messages you marked. You'll find you can now display the message in the Preview Pane.

Views

Outlook Express keeps newsgroup messages on your hard disk for the number of days specified under Tools>Options> Maintenance.

After a few days you'll have downloaded lots of messages. Outlook Express displays the headers of the ones you haven't yet read in a bold font. Messages you have read are listed in a plain font, so you can see the difference. Finding the new ones can still be a chore, though.

1 To make things easier, switch Views so only the messages you haven't read are displayed. To do this, go to View> Current View>Hide Read Messages.

To see only the messages that can be read off-line, select View>Current View> Show Downloaded Messages.

2 To get the older messages back so you can see the new ones in context, select Show All Messages from the same submenu.

Turn on the Views bar (from View> Layout) for quick access to all the different Views.

3 You can also make boring conversations go away. Select the earliest message in the thread, then go to Message> Ignore Conversation.

4 When you set the Current View to Hide Read or Ignored Messages, the entire conversation disappears, regardless of whether you've read the messages.

Message Rules

Message Rules for newsgroups are much like Message Rules for e-mail (see page 165), except they're used to highlight or ignore messages, rather than to file them.

1   Go to Tools>Message Rules>News and click the New button.

2   Choose the conditions. Usually you'll want to specify a newsgroup *and* select one of the other conditions.

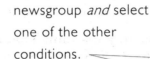

3   Select the action.

4   Click the blue, underlined text to fill in the details.

5   Name the Rule.

If you get fed up with an individual and want to ignore all their messages, select one, then go to Message>Block Sender. Users of other programs call this 'kill-filing'.

6   The Rule is applied to all the messages you receive from now on. This one has filtered out all the messages that don't use the proper format for this group.

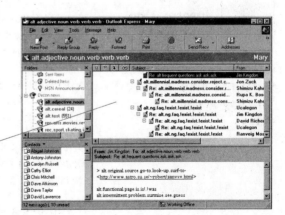

Netiquette

Usenet has a reputation for being hostile to beginners or 'newbies'. While it's true that some groups are hard to break into, most welcome anyone who displays a little common sense and courtesy. In particular, try to adhere to the following guidelines, known collectively as 'netiquette'.

A 'flame' is an abusive message. Some groups tolerate and even encourage flaming; others expect members to be civil. If you post a flame, be prepared to get flamed back!

1   Always read the FAQ (see opposite) before you start posting messages, to avoid (a) posting messages that are inappropriate and (b) asking questions that have already been answered hundreds of times.

2   Avoid posting the same message to several groups at once. This is known as 'cross posting', and it irritates the people who end up downloading your message several times.

3   Don't ever post the same message to lots and lots of newsgroups. This is known as 'spamming', and it irritates everyone. Sadly, you'll encounter lots of spam on Usenet, especially in the `alt` groups. Ignore it – responding just makes things worse.

4   Don't post Rich Text messages (see page 152), because most newsreading software won't display them properly. Stick to Plain Text.

For more information on how to stay in line online, see 'Internet Culture', also in the 'in easy steps' series.

5   If you're replying to a message, don't quote more of the original than is necessary – most people won't want to read it all again. It's helpful to quote the sentence or two you're actually responding to, though.

6   Avoid posting messages that just say, 'Me too,' or, 'I agree.' Wait until you have something more interesting to contribute.

7   Don't type your message in upper case. This is known as SHOUTING, AND IT MAKES YOUR MESSAGE DIFFICULT TO READ.

8   If you use a signature (see page 154), keep it short. Four lines is considered the maximum acceptable length.

FAQs

A FAQ is a compilation of Frequently Asked Questions – and their answers. FAQs exist for two reasons: to set out the newsgroup's scope and rules, and to answer all the questions a newcomer might ask.

'Lurkers' read the messages in a newsgroup, but don't post anything. It's a good way to find out what is acceptable in a particular group.

Most FAQs are posted regularly, generally weekly or monthly. If you 'lurk' in a newsgroup for a while, the FAQ should eventually appear. You can also find FAQs for many newsgroups in the Internet FAQ Archives at:
`http://www.faqs.org/faqs/`

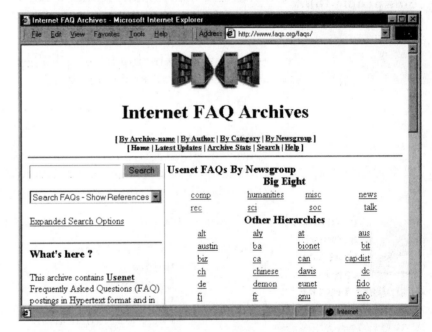

If all else fails, post a polite message asking someone to point you in the right direction. Some groups don't have FAQs; others have more than one, and some FAQs serve several groups. If you can't find a FAQ, lurk for a week or two to get a feel for the group.

Many FAQs represent the collective knowledge of the members of the newsgroup, and they can be fascinating reading in their own right. The question-and-answer format has also become popular elsewhere on the Internet, and Web sites often have FAQ pages.

Smileys and acronyms

Smileys and acronyms speed things up and help you clarify your comments.

Smileys

It's difficult to communicate your emotions in a brief text message to a stranger. This can lead to misunderstandings, particularly if you are prone to bluntness or sarcasm. Consequently, some people use 'smileys' – little faces made out of keyboard characters – to convey their state of mind.

There are many, many smileys. The three you're most likely to encounter are:

:-)	happy
;-)	winking or 'only joking'
:-(	sad or disappointed

(Turn the book through 90 degrees clockwise to see the faces.)

Acronyms

Common phrases are often abbreviated to their initials, producing TLAs (Three-Letter Acronyms) and ETLAs (Extended TLAs). You'll also see phonetic abbreviations.

Common acronyms and abbreviations include:

AFAIK	As far as I know
B4	Before
BTW	By the way
F2F	Face to face
FYI	For your information
<g>	Grin
IMO	In my opinion
IMHO	In my humble opinion
IMNSHO	In my not so humble opinion
ISTM	It seems to me
ISTR	I seem to recall
IRL	In real life (meaning, off the Internet)
L8R	Later
ROFL	Rolling on floor laughing
RSN	Real soon now
RTFM	Read the 'flipping' manual

Index